John H. Ingram

The Philosophy of Handwriting

John H. Ingram

The Philosophy of Handwriting

ISBN/EAN: 9783337236908

Printed in Europe, USA, Canada, Australia, Japan

Cover: Foto ©Thomas Meinert / pixelio.de

More available books at **www.hansebooks.com**

THE
PHILOSOPHY OF HANDWRITING

BY

DON FELIX DE SALAMANCA

'FELIX qui potuit rerum cognoscere causas.'
Virgil.

WITH 135 AUTOGRAPHS

London
CHATTO & WINDUS, PICCADILLY
1879

[The right of translation is reserved.]

TO

THOMAS F. DILLON-CROKER, Esq.

F.S.A., F.R.G.S., &c.

𝔗𝔥𝔦𝔰 𝔙𝔬𝔩𝔲𝔪𝔢 𝔦𝔰 𝔍𝔫𝔰𝔠𝔯𝔦𝔟𝔢𝔡

BY

THE COMMENTATOR

October 1873.

PREFACE.

A FEW YEARS AGO a portion of these sketches appeared, as a series of articles, in the columns of an illustrated contemporary. At the time the idea excited some interest and amusement, and was frequently plagiarised. Much correspondence arose out of the commentary; one of the most distinguished scientists of the age—and a good calligraphist to boot—in acknowledging the justness of the strictures, regretted—in his case needlessly—that he was too old to mend. Other well-known personages desired a niche in the chirographic pantheon. Circumstances having caused a lengthy discontinuance of the series, it is now deemed preferable to publish the whole of the sketches in a volume—after thorough revision—than to resume the original scheme.

Attention may be drawn to the not unnoteworthy fact that whilst, as a rule, Frenchmen are not elegant writers, among their poets—such as Leconte de Lisle, Coppée, Mallarmé, and others noticed in this book—will be found some of the most beautiful living calligraphists of any nation. The knowledge that 'a chiel's amang ye taking notes,' however, may not exercise an altogether unfavourable influence upon English handwriting.

If anyone prove restless under his or her critique, the following words from old Burton's introduction to his 'Anatomie of Melancholy' must be accepted in full of all further explanation :—

'If through weakness, folly, passion, discontent, ignorance, I have said amiss, let it be forgotten and forgiven. I acknowledge that of Tacitus to be true, ' Asperæ facetiæ ubi nimis ex vero traxere, acrem sui memoriam reliquunt ;" and as an honourable man observes, " They fear a satirist's wit, he their memories." I may justly suspect the worst ; and though I hope I have wronged no man, yet in Medea's words I will crave pardon :—

| " —Illud jam voce extrema peto,
Ne si qua noster dubius effudit
    dolor,
Maneant in animo verba, sed
    melior tibi.
Memoria nostri subeat, hæc iræ
    data
Obliterentur"— | " And in my last words this I do
    desire,
That what in passion I have said,
    or ire,
May be forgotten, and a better
    mind
Be had of us, hereafter as you
    find." |

*   *   *   *   *

'If thou knewest my modesty and simplicity, thou wouldst easily pardon and forgive what is here amiss, or

by thee misconceived. If hereafter anatomising this
surly humour, my hand slip, as an unskilful 'prentice I
lance too deep, and cut through skin, and all at unawares,
make it smart, or cut awry, pardon a rude hand, an unskilful knife, 'tis a most difficult thing to keep an even
tone, a perpetual tenor, and not sometimes to lash out ;
difficile est Satyram non scribere, there be so many objects
to divert, inward perturbations to molest, and the very
best may sometimes err. . . . But what needs all this?
I hope there will no such cause of offence be given, . . .
but I presume of *thy* good favour and gracious acceptance
[gentle reader]. Out of an assured hope and confidence
thereof, I will begin.'

FELIX DE SALAMANCA.

CONTENTS.

	PAGE
About, Edmond	9
Ainsworth, W. Harrison	10
Albery, James	11
Alma-Tadema, L.	12
Arnold, Matthew	13
Banville, Théodore de	14
Barbier, Auguste	15
Beaconsfield, Earl of, vide Disraeli, B.	44
Beauregard, G. T.	16
Benedict, Sir Julius	17
Bennett, Sir William Sterndale	18
Blind, Karl	19
Bonheur, R.	20
Boucicault, Dion	21
Braddon, M. E.	22
Bright, John	24
Madox-Brown, Ford	25
Browning, Robert	26
Bryant, W. C.	27
Byron, Henry J.	28
Carlyle, T.	29
Clemens, Samuel L. ('Mark Twain')	30
Cobden, Richard	31

	PAGE
COLENSO, J. W.	32
COLLINS, WILKIE	33
COOK, ELIZA	35
COPPÉE, FRANÇOIS	36
COSTA, MICHAEL	37
CRAIG, ISA	38
DARWIN, C.	39
DAUDET, ALPHONSE	41
DAVIS, JEFFERSON	42
DILKE, SIR CHARLES WENTWORTH	43
DISRAELI, B.	44
DORAN, J.	46
DORÉ, G.	47
DUMAS, A., PÈRE	48
DUMAS, A., FILS	49
FAITHFULL, EMILY	50
FERGUSSON, SIR WILLIAM	51
FREEMAN, EDWARD A.	52
FREILIGRATH, F.	53
GARIBALDI, G.	54
GAUTIER, THÉOPHILE	55
GLADSTONE, W. E.	56
GLATIGNY, ALBERT	57
GOSSE, EDMUND W.	58
GOUNOD, CHARLES	59
GUIZOT, F.	60
HALLIDAY, ANDREW	61
HARTE, BRET	62
HERVÉ	63
HOLMES, O. W.	64
HORNE, R. H.	65
HUGO, VICTOR	66
HUXLEY, T. H.	68

	PAGE
IGNATIUS	69
JACKSON, T. J. ('STONEWALL')	70
JOHNSTONE, J. E.	71
KINGSLEY, REV. C.	72
KOSSUTH, L.	73
LEE, R. E.	74
LELAND, CHARLES G.	75
LESSEPS, COUNT FERDINAND DE	76
GOLDSCHMIDT, JENNY LIND-	77
LYNTON, E. LYNN	78
LISLE, LECONTE DE	79
LIVINGSTONE, DAVID	80
LOCKER, F.	81
LONGFELLOW, HENRY W.	82
LOWELL, J. R.	84
LUBBOCK, SIR JOHN	85
LYTTON, LORD	86
MᶜCARTHY, JUSTIN	87
MALLARMÉ, STÉPHANE	88
MALLOCK, W. H.	89
MANET, EDWARD	90
MANNING, CARDINAL H. E.	91
MARSTON, WESTLAND	92
MARTIN, THEODORE	93
MAZZINI, JOSEPH	94
MENDÈS, CATULLE	95
MILL, J. S.	96
MILLAIS, JOHN EVERETT	97
MORRIS, WILLIAM	99
MUSSET, ALFRED DE	100
NEWMAN, CARDINAL JOHN H.	101
NORTON, C. (LADY STIRLING-MAXWELL)	102
OFFENBACH, C.	103

	PAGE
PATTI, ADELINA	104
O'SHAUGHNESSY, ARTHUR	105
'OUIDA'	106
OWEN, RICHARD	107
PAGET, SIR JAMES	108
PAYN, JAMES	109
PAYNE, JOHN	110
PROCTOR, R. A.	111
PRUDHOMME, SULLY	112
READE, CHARLES	113
REEVES, SIMS	114
REGNAULT, HENRI	115
RICHARDS, ALFRED B.	116
RICHARDSON, R. W.	117
RISTORI, ADELAIDE	118
ROSSETTI, CHRISTINA G.	119
ROSSETTI, D. G.	120
ROSSETTI, W. M.	121
RUSKIN, J.	122
SALA, GEORGE AUGUSTUS	123
SAND,' 'GEORGE	124
SANDEAU, JULES	125
SANTLEY, C.	126
SAWYER, WILLIAM	127
SCHLIEMANN	129
SIMON, JULES	130
STANLEY, HENRY M.	131
'STELLA'	132
STEPHEN, LESLIE	133
SPURGEON, REV. C. H.	134
SULLIVAN, ARTHUR S.	135
SWINBURNE, A. C.	136
TAYLOR, SIR HENRY	137

	PAGE
TAYLOR, TOM	138
TENNYSON, A.	139
THIERS, A.	140
THOMPSON, SIR HENRY	141
THORNBURY, WALTER	142
TROLLOPE, ANTHONY	143
TYNDALL, JOHN	144
'TWAIN,' 'MARK, *vide* CLEMENS, S. L.	30
VERDI, G.	146
WAGNER, R.	147
WALKER, MARY E., M.D.	148
WHITMAN, WALT	149
WHITTIER, JOHN G.	151
WOOD, ELLEN	152
ZOLA, EMILE	153

THE
Philosophy of Handwriting.

CHIROMANCY, says Monsieur Desbarrolles, in his learned little work on 'Les Mystères de la Main,' is as old as the world. Like so many other Asian mysteries, it is supposed to have emanated from India. Long lost to the wise, the art was recovered by an erudite Hebrew, and 'thanks to his indications,' says the French savant, 'we have studied one by one all the works written on Chiromancy, and by the aid of comparison sought to extract the truth from the midst of numerous errors.'

To probe so deeply into the mere history of this ancient and recondite study as did M. Desbarrolles, is not my present purpose, nor is it my intention to cite from the many 'quaint and curious volumes' that have been written upon the subject of Chiromancy more than will be sufficient to establish the truth of my proposition that a strong analogy does exist between a man's personal character and his calligraphy. For the benefit of those, however, who would wish to pry more closely into the abstruse mysteries of this occult science, and would like to see for themselves that my theory is neither new nor without learned supporters, the following little known works—when obtainable—may be recommended as useful : 'Die Chiromanten-Kunst' of Lustlieb, a very singular tome of only twenty-six leaves, and of which no perfect copy is known to be in existence; Michael Scot's 'Hande Boke of Autographye;' and Dr. John Lee's 'Treatyse offe chyrographye : wythe ane artefulle and most pleasante wanderynge ine thee delectable maze of chyromancye.' 'Chiromancie Dévoilée,' by the Sieur de Galimatias, although so frequently alluded to by Dr. Lee, is merely a brochure of seven pages, and is only valuable for its references to rare and, in some instances, unknown tomes, none of which are mentioned by Dibden or Brunet. The most interesting of the works therein referred to would appear to be the 'Flores Divinas de Ciromancia,' by El Señor Doctor Cilla of the University of Salamanca, and an exquisitely written manuscript in the library of the Vatican, the handiwork, seemingly, of a Paduan priest. The value of this latter work is greatly enhanced by the numerous authentic autographs—many of which are very scarce and some, apparently, unique—which it contains. Thus much *pour les savants*.

For the general reader the veritable autograph of a celebrated person will, of itself, be of sufficient interest without any extraneous aid from chiromancy. An autograph may generally be accepted as truly characteristic of its writer. It is often written more carefully—always more fluently—than the remainder of his manuscript; and from these very circumstances—from the extra care, deliberateness, and frequency of its use—acquires a settled form that better portrays its author's idiosyncrasies than could any quantity of his other writing. 'The handwriting bears an analogy to the character of the writer,' the elder D'Israeli remarks, 'as all voluntary actions are characteristic.' One has only to ponder over the strength of those fluctuating feelings which pass from the heart or brain into the fingers—impelling them to reveal or conceal the thoughts of the scribe—to feel that it is not claiming too much to claim for them the power of imprinting some 'touch of nature' on the page—some touch by which the adept may be more or less guided to a comprehension of the writer's character. Of course it is not always the workmanship of the best scribe that is easiest for the chiromancer to unriddle, any more than the artist finds his best models in the prettiest faces. Hawthorne observes, in an unknown essay of his on Autographs, 'There are said to be temperaments endowed with sympathies so exquisite that, by merely handling an autograph they can detect the writer's character with unerring accuracy, and read his inmost heart as easily as a less gifted eye would peruse the written page.' Without pretending to such preternatural discernment as that shadowed forth by the author of 'The Scarlet Letter,' the longer I study chiromancy the more assured do I become of its value and utility.

It has been declared that next to seeing a distinguished man we desire to see his portrait and, after that, his autograph. But an autograph has this advantage over a portrait, *it must be faithful*, which a portrait rarely is. In perusing the veritable handwriting of a celebrated person we seem brought into personal contact with him, and are ready to exclaim with Calderon, in his inimitable 'Secreto a voces :'—

> What, his autograph !—his letter !
> Every line his own handwriting !

In his above mentioned essay Hawthorne—alluding to the autographs of distinguished people—says that 'the words may come to us as with the living utterance of one of those illustrious men speaking face to face, in friendly communion. Strange,' he continues, 'that the mere identity of paper and ink should be so powerful. The same thoughts might look cold and ineffectual in a printed book. Human nature craves a certain materialism, and clings pertinaciously to what is tangible, as if that were of more importance than the spirit accidentally involved in it. And, in truth, the original manuscript has always something which print itself must inevitably lose. An erasure, even a blot, a casual irregularity of hand, and all such little imperfections of mechanical execution, bring us close to the writer, and perhaps convey some of those subtle intimations for which language has no shape.'

Granting all this, it may be urged, the autographs of famous personages are not so readily obtainable as are their portraits. Anyone, at any time, by buying a photograph or an illustrated paper can procure the desiderated portrait, but few are enabled to obtain the signature of the distinguished man or woman. The celebrated are justly tenacious of their handwriting, and even professional autograph-mongers often find them as difficult to 'draw out' as a fox that has run to ground. From me—from Felix de Salamanca—as one of themselves, the notable never find it in their hearts to refuse the requested line. As well, therefore, as pointing a moral by the choice specimens of autography herein depicted, I can make the multitude partakers of my treasures, and, by placing them within the reach of all, save the many the trouble of asking for autographs and the 'great' few the anguish of withholding them.

Those autographs which are now placed before the reader are all of more or less distinguished individuals—in most cases of individuals whose reputation is not likely to prove ephemeral—and are, therefore, worthy preservation. In order to afford wider interest and variety to this theme, this collection will not be confined to the calligraphy of *literati* only, or, indeed, to any one class of persons, but will include *facsimile* signatures of people distinguished in various professions. As a rule, the autographs of only living persons, as most typical of our time, will be included, but, when equally representative, those of persons recently departed from among us will also be given. For reasons which are obvious, this little book will be only a selection—although a selection from the most eminent—of the signatures of celebrated contemporaries, and those of many persons of distinction must necessarily be excluded. This exclusion should not be deemed a desire to overlook or disparage any particular personage's claims to fame, but as chiefly caused by the peculiar nature of the work.

It must not be imagined that the conclusions as to character herein arrived at have been deduced from autographs alone: they are the result of a careful inspection of each person's correspondence—in some instances from quite a large quantity of it. A portion of this said correspondence, moreover, a Chabot might find difficult to decipher, so illegible and carelessly executed is, frequently, the calligraphy of those people whose desire or duty it is to instruct mankind. *They* should at least know how to form their 'pothooks and hangers,' even if they do not mind their 'ps' and 'qs.' If the dictum of Rogers be correct, that the man who writes his name obscurely is guilty of impertinence to the person addressed, what an impertinent class celebrated people must be! Quite two-thirds of them write as if obscurity were the one thing needful, whilst a large proportion of them—especially those who are known not to have any superfluous time—waste the precious moments by indulging in various kinds of calligraphical *flourishes*. Even among those most literary of the *literati*—the poets—this inexcusable vulgarity occasionally breaks out.

Although—to invert the old saying, *le vraisemblable n'est pas toujours le vrai*—the chirographical performances of men secluded from the hurry and turmoil of the outer world may reasonably be supposed to have a finish in style and impress of individuality utterly unattainable by the handwriting of toilers in more hurried pursuits: accustomed to jot down hasty notes in the midst of his daily avocations, and to make use of any implement obtainable, the lawyer or the physician acquires speedily a style—or want of style—totally at variance with that ordained for him by nature or previous education. Editorial urgency, also, frequently ruins a man's calligraphy, and reduces it to an anything but fortuitous conglomeration of ciphers, beyond the skill of a Champollion to interpret. Yet, when it be considered that 'one shade the more, one shade the less,' ofttimes makes all the difference between the legible and the incomprehensible, and that, indeed, the addition of a single comma once made a man's legacy ten thousand francs less, the importance of writing clearly, and punctuating correctly—an art almost unknown—is apparent. The importance of handwriting has been promptly recognised and carefully guarded by the legislature, which, indeed, attaches more value to a simple signature than to the personal testimony of numerous witnesses, and permits a dead man's autograph to make or mar the future happiness of his fellows. Should not this alone cause writers to heed the manner of their calligraphy?

A strong resemblance is ofttimes discernible between the handwritings of various members of a family, especially after practice has caused the style to become settled. D'Israeli says that 'to every individual Nature has given a distinct sort of writing, as she has given them a peculiar countenance, voice, and manner;' and it is but completing the analogy to point out how Nature has, also, given family resemblances in all these peculiarities. Indeed, it is not overstraining the limits of this theme to assert that not only are the idiosyncrasies of individual scribes proclaimed by their penmanship, but even the peculiarities of whole nations. *Par exemple*, the writing of a Frenchman is generally florid, almost feverish in its *petit*, fantastic formations, whilst a commercial carefulness distinguishes the calligraphy of the reflective Teuton. The Italian is of a finer but less forcible type than the French, but has many features of similarity, as has, indeed, the manuscript of the whole Latin race.

'I am a sort of believer in handwriting divination,' said the late Mrs. Browning, 'and took interest in *the very shapes of their respective alphabets*;' and those versed in hieroglyphic languages well know how much wisdom and truth are contained in these words of the great poetess.

It is to be hoped that none of my lady readers—or writers—will find fault with me for the comments hereinafter, with all due deference, made upon their handiwork. Truthfully, it must be stated that, as a rule, women do not write so well as men, nor take such pains with their calligraphy; and, although, generally having more leisure, are fond of subscribing themselves 'in haste,' 'hastily,' and 'in great haste.' Women, however, ignore all those egotistic affectations which the self-styled 'lords of creation' are so fond of indulging in, in the foolish hope that their assumed peculiarities will be mistaken for the eccentricities of genius. No woman could be such an ass as Leo Allatius was, as to use the same pen for forty years, in hopes of having the fact recorded in some future 'Curiosities of Literature;' nor act so absurdly as did that translator of 'Pliny' who only used one pen over his work, for the sole purpose, apparently, of being thereby enabled to commemorate the feat in this doggerel rhyme :—

> With one sole pen I wrote this book,
> Made of a grey goose quill;
> A pen it was when it I took,
> A pen I leave it still.

The letters of Edmond About have a sharp irritable flavour about them, strongly suggestive of mosquito stings. Generally, his capitals are only somewhat magnified copies of his smaller letters; his finals rarely attain full growth, and—undeveloped *fœtus* that they are—may be deemed to appertain *à l'état de lettre morte*. His signature is larger and better manufactured than the remainder of his handwriting, of which, however, it is equally characteristic. Maimed and maltreated as the members of Monsieur About's alphabetical family are, they are generally legible, being clearly and cleanly made. There is no marked originality about the style, which is that of the multitude, and more suggestive of a *décoré* than that of a genius—not, perhaps, of a Monsieur Prud'homme precisely, but scarcely that of a great author. It would be difficult to assign any particular individuality to a man inditing so conventional a style of chirography, unless, indeed, a spice of sarcastic humour might be detected in its fluent evolutions.

W. Harrison Ainsworth

The author of 'Mervyn Clitheroe,' and two dozen or more of those books found in every schoolboy's locker, indites a very characteristic hand, and one that in its unwavering firmness gives no hint of the threescore years and fourteen placed to its credit by the biographers. The general manuscript has a somewhat feminine air, but the letters are more rounded in form, and have more decision than have those manufactured by members of the fair sex. As a rule, each letter is legibly finished without any approach to the indecency of flourish, but some few—especially the 'y'—suffer an amputation of the loop, whilst in other cases that letter is indistinguishable from 'g.' The signature agrees in every respect with the body of the manuscript, a very clear proof that its author eschews affectation. A neat, nervous, and pleasant chirography to peruse is that written by Mr. Harrison Ainsworth, and one that inspires genial visions of its composer. Without the slightest *soupçon* of offensive egotism, it betrays a self-consciousness of the fact that the writer has a name not quite unknown in the Temple of Fame, and that he is by no means dissatisfied with his knowledge thereanent. Moreover it has the air of being the work of a gentleman.

Many readers would be pleased with this author's signature. The author of 'The Pink Dominoes' does not, as a rule, dot his 'i' nor cross his 't,' and, altogether, indites a somewhat commercial-looking style of calligraphy. Although there is a general *vraisemblance* pervading his writing, his letters are very unequal in height and shape; his 'e' cannot be distinguished from his 'i.' and many other of the *soi-disant* 'minor morals' of chirography are neglected or outraged. The present autograph is a fair specimen of his skill.

To 'gild refined gold' may well be an idle task, but we cannot be too grateful to the hand 'which doth even Beauty beautify.' And how frequently has Mr. Alma-Tadema performed this labour of love for us! But as he has thus acted in great things, may we also expect equal proficiency in minor matters? It is difficult for the hand to forget its cunning, therefore it is not surprising to discover that our true artists, even when they ignore our calligraphical rules, and offend against all scriptorial proprieties, indite a style which in picturesqueness and originality far outvalues any scores of exact, clerkly, commonplace, modes. As might be expected, Mr. Alma-Tadema by no means adheres to the rules and routine of conventional chirography. The slope of his letters is not uniform, and the rather inclines backwards than forwards; punctuation—that *bête noire* of the unliterary!—is ignored; many of his words halt, as if their inditer were doubtful whether to express them or not; his 'e' is an undotted 'i;' and other defects mar the general tenour of his manuscript. But the letters are all legible, the words compact, and, as a rule, the finals carefully finished; so that, altogether, Mr. Alma-Tadema's power to beautify Beauty might much more safely be predicated from his chirography than from most of his brethren's.

If ever an author's handwriting typified his literary character, then does Matthew Arnold's his. Clear, classic, cold, and as neatly penned as anyone could wish, it is easy to believe its writer to be a man of taste, of talent, and of high educational qualifications, but scarcely a genius, and not without a slight suspicion of dogmatism. Among the faults of Mr. Arnold's style of writing may be noted the propensity he has of placing the dot at a preposterous distance from the 'i' and the crosses from their 'ts.' His letters are too angular to suit our taste.

De Banville's motto should be *multum in parvo*, for he contrives to compress as many words into a few pages of manuscript as would make another 'Decameron.' The author of 'Les Odes Funambulesques' would be the man to get the Iliad into a nutshell, although his petit penmanship is more suggestive of Petronius Arbiter's 'chaste Latinity' than the thunder-riving characters of Homeric Greek. The alphabetical symbols of Cadmus were of Bœotian rudeness, but our poet's calligraphy is of exquisite neatness. If his letters are so tiny that they might have been used in the correspondence of Titania's court, they are delightfully legible, and all completely fashioned after their kind—which kind is both original and elegant. Whether de Banville could so far rival St. Theodosius as to write out all the Gospels in letters of gold, without a single error or blot, only the attempt would show, but as yet all his manuscript seen by us is as immaculate as Joseph. His signature is somewhat inferior in style to the rest of his correspondence, but is very characteristic of the *riante bonhomie* we should feel inclined to ascribe him, after a crucial examination of his fantastic chirography.

Knowing no man whose aspirations we honour more than those of the author of the 'Rimes Héroïques,' and perusing his letters with reverence, there is almost a feeling of dread within us lest we should for the nonce forget the stern dicta of our art, and speak too warmly of the calligraphy of him who said :—

> Un brave homme est pour moi chose belle et touchante,
> Qu'il sorte du bas peuple ou descende des rois ;
> Quand je vois un brave homme, aussitôt je le chante
> Du profond de mon cœur et du fort de ma voix.

But the critique shall not be foregone. Auguste Barbier, whose signature is not so well executed as the body of his epistolary documents, indites a charming, clear, and poetic style, albeit somewhat too small. A leading peculiarity is the 'l,' which is shaped like a capital 'S ;' another, and not so original a peculiarity, being the 'c'-shaped 'b,' as seen in the *facsimile*. Our poet is also accustomed to use the literary *delta* for 'd.' The whole of his calligraphy is most carefully, neatly, and yet flowingly executed, the unlooped 'g' in the signature being quite an exception, as is also the somewhat indefinite flourish in the surname. The eccentrically shaped 'B' is worth notice, as a symbol of the care and thought expended upon even so, apparently, trivial a thing in a man's career as is his autograph.

General Beauregard's calligraphy is the clearest and most legible of those Confederate chieftains who held the Northern States at bay, although it is not so pleasing to professional critics as that of General Johnston. The famous West Point Superintendent and Fort Sumter assailant indulges in a little chirographical flourishing that could not be permitted in a meaner man, but his letters are neatly and carefully rounded, and finished off to the ultimate stroke. The mannerism is that of a straightforward person having nothing to conceal, but not ill disposed towards the pomp of office. Like too many of his countrymen's, General Beauregard's chirographical productions are replete with fine hair lines, the which deprive the manuscript of nearly all characteristicality. Nevertheless, this hand is by no means an unhandsome one, and is superior to his brother-general's in uniformity of slope.

The same fondness for flourish which disfigures the writing of so many musical celebrities, spoils Benedict's otherwise pleasant hand. Although by birth a German, he has very fairly mastered the English method of building *Buchstaben*, and indites a good, close, condensed, and somewhat literary-looking sort of calligraphy. The most noticeable faults in such of his epistles as have reached our hands are, inability to form the English 's;' a very *un*-German absence of punctuation; flourishes, instead of loops, to the 'ys;' and an occasional attempt to cheat a letter out of its fair share of pothooks and hangers, which is a sin only second to that of an artist who depicts an animal minus its proper number of limbs. It is simply ridiculous to put a little wriggle for 'r,' or make a twist do duty for 't.' These failures notwithstanding, we do not dislike the *Handschrift* of Sir Julius: it is indicative of strongmindedness, perseverance, and a thorough belief in his own powers.

[signature: William Sterndale Bennett]

A plain matter-of-fact style, devoid of all needless embellishment, is the handwriting of Sir William Sterndale Bennett. The signature is somewhat better formed, and has, indeed, a more decided or practised appearance than the remainder of the manuscript, the whole of which, however, is invariably clear and readable, with no nearer approach to a flourish than the cross of the 't' in the autograph. As a rule, musicians are not the best of writers, but this is a very distinct specimen of calligraphy, and gives one the idea of having been indited by a thoroughly reliable man, which view is strengthened by the carefulness of the address and dating. Punctuation is eschewed. Clearness, without much beauty, is the distinguishing *trait* of Sir William's chirography.

Der ist allein ein freier Mann . . .
Der sie sich *selbst* verdienen kann,

sang Herwegh years ago, and his countryman, Karl Blind, has taken the truth well to heart, and has deserved, if not obtained, success. His calligraphy is one of the most manly, straightforward, and energetic hands in this *Sammlung*. The style is terse, decided, and sufficiently original for a poet, although somewhat more fluent than that *genus* of beings generally indulges in. No studied peculiarity or mannerism—save in the wonderful contortions of the flourish after the signature—detract from the quaint simplicity of this writing, the most noticeable thing about the letters being the singular force by which each one appears to have been ended: not a single stroke is deficient, but each member of the alphabet ends abruptly—instantaneously—upon arrival at a certain point. This is quite different from the method of nearly all chirographists, who either begin too soon or end too late: Karl Blind has struck upon the happy medium. The signature is somewhat larger and more strained than the rest of his *Handschrift*, which is, taken all in all, a very handsome one, and indicative of severe independence.

According to Kit Marlowe, when Hero played upon her lute, the air

> In twenty sweet forms danced about her fingers;

and some may deem Mademoiselle Rosa Bonheur's calligraphy equally memorable, for, to a certainty, it dances about her pages in forms innumerable; but whether 'sweet' is questionable. Some of her strokes are most artistic and picturesque, and give a most animated, but not very easily decipherable, appearance to her manuscript. Her flourishes are veritable lines of beauty, but they are not handwriting. *Sans le mot d'énigme* few folk would be able to unriddle the mystery enveloped in her signature. That a capital 'B' was represented by that Ammonite-horned 'hanger,' or that a *bonheur* was symbolized by the *tout ensemble* of those curves and curls, would only be guessed by a Chabot or Champollion. And the autograph is representative of the general style; only a few letters are legible, and even those few are not correctly formed. Beyond an intense love of bold design and of a somewhat defiant *bravura*, it would scarcely be safe to predicate aught of this writer's character from her penmanship.

The author of the 'Colleen Bawn' writes a very clear and somewhat clerkly hand, the letters of the signature being larger and better formed than the rest of his communications. His capital letters are very uncertain; sometimes the 'S' is made like 'L,' and sometimes the 'I' and the 'C' are made alike. Mr. Boucicault's calligraphy, with a little careful manipulation, would become a fair mercantile hand, but its inditer would have to forego his abbreviations. He is very fond of running two words into one, omits all the most necessary punctuation, and is not without a certain amount of tremulousness in his strokes, especially towards the end of his letters. But few of his 'ts' are crossed, or his 'is' dotted, yet his words are clearly made, and his communications very neatly paragraphed. Although Horace will not allow mediocrity to poets, this writer's motto in literature would be, doubtless, and appropriately, *medio tutissimus ibis*. A perceptive eye for good situations, and a sufficient experience of life to make the most of its transient characteristics, might be safely predicated of such a writer, but beyond that it would be unsafe to venture.

Miss Braddon writes pretty fair *copy* for the printers, in a vigorous, masculine manner, and her letters are, certainly, so far based upon scholastic injunctions that the upstrokes are light and the downstrokes are heavy. But the handwriting of the authoress of 'Lady Audley's Secret,' apart from its general hastiness and ultra-dashiness of look, is wofully deficient in the minor morals of chirography. Numberless are the letters left unfinished, words contracted, and similarities made between normally dissimilar letters: 'k' and 'h' are made exactly alike; so are 'o' and 'i;' and but too frequently 'e' is only the latter without the dot. Some of her capitals are handsome specimens of calligraphy, whilst others are very defective. She has a variety of capital 'Ms,' but between the one proceeding downwards from above the line and her capital 'B' there is a close resemblance that is most unnatural. Some of her contractions—such as 'yrs.' for 'yours,' and 'yr.' for 'your'—may be taken as indefensible examples of what not even haste could be urged in palliation of. Although the slope of her letters is fairly uniform, the distance between the lines varies considerably. All these minutiæ contribute not only towards an attractive mode of handwriting, but also towards affording a generally fair idea of the writer's character. It is owing to the various blemishes alluded to that the calligraphy of Miss Braddon is anything but easy for casual readers to comprehend, and yet it is impossible to disregard the fact that a very slight amount of extra care on this writer's part would result in a splendid although somewhat unimaginative style. Miss Braddon could, if she would, indite a superb hand. Her epistles actually sparkle with brilliant combinations of 'pothooks and hangers,' and, placed beside those of most of her literary *consœurs*, excel them in the same way that a glass of sparkling Cliquot does a goblet of still Burgundy.

The autograph of John Bright is one of unpretentious strength and simplicity. In many respects it resembles the style in which Mr. Gladstone wrote previous to the introduction of post-cards, but is rather more vigorous. There is little grace and still less picturesqueness about the writing, but it is characteristic of a straightforward, decided temperament, not quite unalloyed with a spice of self esteem. The Machiavellian arts of diplomancy are in no way detectable in such calligraphy. The signature is thoroughly representative of the whole style, the *form* of which is far from perfection. The 'e' is only an 'i,' as is, indeed, but too often the 'o.' The 'f' is minus its girdle, being turned up like the unlooped 'g' in the autograph. One word is often linked on to the next, and many other minor defects are apparent in the whole manuscript, the manner of which might be termed Parliamentary, so general is it with the purely political members of the House of Commons.

Lord Bacon's advice, 'Stay a little, that we may make an end the sooner,' does not, apparently, much impress this famous artist when a letter has to be designed. The man whose 'Work' is of world-wide reputation certainly does not love to labour at the calligraphic art, but dashes off his epistles *currente calamo*. Although Mr. Madox-Brown's letters are fairly legible, especially to those acquainted with their style, their hasty appearance troubles one with the idea that to execute them must have quite worried their inditer, and their completion have lifted a burden off his mind. Frankly, this chirography is a picturesque and suggestive one, but one that could be rendered far better did its author deem it worth the while to devote the time expended in flourish to a somewhat more elaborate manipulation of his letters, and contrive to retain a respectable stylus for general use, instead of contenting himself with any implement available. Certain aberrations, if not allowed to, are indulged in by, genius, and amongst those to which Mr. Madox-Brown would have to plead guilty—so far as calligraphy is concerned—are ignored punctuation, omitted dates, and sundry other infringements of the *lex non scripta*. But this artist's handwriting is very variable, and his signature varies with the rest of his manuscript, being, apparently, more influenced by the implement made use of than by the temperament of the inditer. A frank, kindly, ingenuous disposition must inspire the author of this autography.

Robert Browning writes as a poet should write. His manuscript is thoroughly emblematic of his poetry, and is distinguished by as many traits that casual observers might overlook as are his poems. His calligraphy is small but clearly formed, the most prominent peculiarity being the frequency with which the different syllables of a word are disconnected from each other. For example, 'poetical' is written 'poe ti cal,' as if it were three words. Sometimes, but not often, he makes the sign '&' instead of writing the conjunction, but this is not in accordance with his general artistic care, and may be regarded as the exception rather than the rule. In his correspondence the words are as neatly finished, and his letters are as carefully punctuated, as if prepared for the press. Were his beautiful chirography placed before us as that of a stranger, we should at once pronounce it not only that of a distinguished man, but also of one who never did anything carelessly.

For a young clerk seeking a situation, Bryant's handwriting might prove a recommendation, but for a poet, and that the author of 'June' must have been, it is most disappointing. Towards the latter days of the veteran author's life, and after he had presumedly forborne to pursue the Muses, his chirography assumed a more manly and decided style, but during the greater part of his lengthy career it was simply horrible, and did not intimate the slightest scintillation of genius. Letters all sloping in different directions, fine hair lines, half a dozen words looped on to one another, and, worse than all, a multitudinous array of flourishes, gave Bryant's manuscript an execrable appearance. All these calligraphical fanfaronades in a literary man are heartrending, and cast grave doubts on his genius. There is no beauty and nothing but commonplaceness about every specimen of Bryant's correspondence that has yet come under our ken.

A fluent but not too legible pen is wielded by the author of 'Our Boys.' Mr. Byron's calligraphy is professional in style and gentlemanly in appearance, but is not indicative of any great range of power; yet, in the words of the sage, Periander, Μελέτη τὸ πᾶν ('Everything can be accomplished by care and industry'). His letters are too angular for an Englishman's, and too curtailed to receive any great chirographical praise. His 't' is often left uncrossed and his 'i' undotted : he writes as if he did not care whether the recipient of his epistle valued it or not, and in a hasty but trenchant manner. The inditer of such a hand might well be the author of works teeming with wit and *espièglerie*, but the summit of Olympus is far beyond his flight.

The chirography of 'the Chelsea Philosopher' is not a very commendable one, although it has safely steered clear of the sandbank of Conventionality. In his handiwork there is too much evident effort at effect—too palpable an attempt at originality—for it to pass current as pure inspiration. His epistles are neatly paragraphed and carefully punctuated, as if prepared for the printer, and although for several years past the letters have been somewhat shaky, they are not difficult to decipher. Eccentric and spiteful-looking little flourishes dart about his manuscript in various odd ways : some are intended to represent the 'i' dot, although far removed from their parent stem, whilst others, commenced as a cross to the 't,' suddenly recoil in an absurd fashion, as if attempting a calligraphical somersault, and in so doing occasionally cancel the entire word whence they sprang. Some letters slope one way, and some another ; some are halt, maimed, or crippled ; whilst many are unequal in height, form, style, and everything else. The autograph is rather larger than the rest of the manuscript, the manner of which does not impress the eye pleasantly, its crabbed look not being very significant of amability.

Mark Twain's note of hand, if not of very elaborate construction, is fairly symbolic of the *littérateur*, who does not trouble himself overscrupulously about the minutiæ of his profession. His is a fluent, business-like, and legible style, somewhat large and conventional, like the majority of his countrymen's. It is free from flourish, and all the letters are correctly shaped, being neither deformed nor quaint in construction. No possessor of the divine afflatus, of course, ever indited such a hand, but many a successful speculator in Wall Street may have done so. Mr. Clemens is not the man to make his autograph different from the remainder of his manuscript. It is thoroughly characteristic of a shrewd man of the world.

The great Freetrader, whose patriotic exertions made his country richer by untold millions, indited a handsome masculine hand, well worthy of his fame. Although at times modified in form and with some of the letters left unfinished under pressure of circumstances, Cobden's writing was always fluent, bold, and thoroughly legible, and quite unmarked by pert flourish or mercantile contractions. His manuscript is simple, but not bald; forcible, but not graceful. The words are properly spaced, but are not uniform in slope, nor are they punctuated. Some of the capitals are elegantly shaped, and the finals frequently well formed and always decided. The celebrated Corn Law Reformer's chirography is neither suggestive of a poet nor a pedler, but it is that of a man endowed with a strong will, self-respect, and freedom from all affectation.

If an unsophisticated Zulu were enabled to shake this right reverend gentleman's belief in some of the dogmas of his faith, what may not a learned European professor be enabled to do with regard to the items of his chirographical art? Frankly, however, it must be conceded that Bishop Colenso indites a much more legible and masculine hand than is usual with the high dignitaries of his own or any other person's Church. In most respects the Bishop's style strongly resembles that of Mr. John Bright, its chief divergence being its superiority in compactness—evidence of literary experience. Many of Colenso's letters, especially his capitals, are very elegantly shaped, as is, indeed, to be seen in the thoroughly representative signature. Punctuation, dating, and all those valuable 'trifles' which constitute a reliable correspondent, are most logically carried out. The chief faults in Bishop Colenso's method of handwriting is the frequent omission or suppression of some essential portion of a letter—a pothook or hanger of vital logical importance often being absent—otherwise it is a fluent, dignified, graceful style, somewhat above the usual mediocrity of a public personage's, yet, by reason of its conventionality and exemption from quaintness, somewhat below the mannerism of *literati* and artists.

A straightforward, manly, but not very original or artistic style, is that indited by Wilkie Collins. Very few of his alphabetical retainers but have suffered the loss of one limb or the other: one is deficient a top, another a tail, whilst a third is minus an arm, or, perchance, has not a leg to stand upon. Like so many of his *confrères*, Mr. Collins makes no distinction between the 'n' and the 'u,' consequently, when two or more of those letters come into combination—as they so frequently do in the English language—it is somewhat difficult to decipher his meaning; and, indeed, he himself, in the confusion of so many similar up and down strokes, has been known to give a word more pothooks than appertained to it legally. The second curve of the 'n' or 'm' should proceed from the top or shoulder, and not be carried up, as in the 'u,' from the line. This may seem a trifle, but these trifles may have ruined a Shakespearean thought or Miltonic theme; and one such is stated to have given rise to a costly lawsuit between Mr. London and Mr. Loudon, to decide which of the two was the party named in the will of a gentleman in whose handwriting the letters in question were made alike. Such a word as *muniment*, written in the usual manner of the author of 'The Woman in White,' would puzzle the analytic faculties of

an Edgar Poe, or the Gerome Nani mentioned by
Pancirollus as so skilled in calligraphical ciphers that he
solved all that were brought to him, 'though never so
hard and abstruse.' Apart from these defects, and putting
on one side insufficiency of punctuation, the chirography
of Mr. Wilkie Collins is not, by any means, an unpleasing
one, it having a masculine, honest air. The autograph
is typical of the general manuscript.

Dumas *père* said that all people who wrote backwards wrote alike; but if this be the rule, Eliza Cook is an exception to it: she writes backwards, yet she does not write like anybody else, but in a thoroughly original style. The epistle from which the accompanying autograph is taken differs from her general method in having all the strokes of the letters of a uniform thickness, whereas her writing usually is formed of alternate thick and thin, or hair, strokes. Her 'd' is always the Greek *delta*; her 'i' is rarely dotted; her words sometimes run into one another; and many of her letters are incomplete. She punctuates, dates, and heads her communications, but often signs them with initials only. She cannot forbear from the luxury of a flourish in the signature, which is a very fair specimen of her general hand. A leading peculiarity, thoroughly characteristic of her independence of thought, is the invariably placing the superscriptory sentence of her communications after, instead of—according to common custom—before the first paragraph. Thus, instead of beginning, 'My dear Don Felix,' she would commence, 'I am extremely pleased you are carrying your project in triumph, my dear Don Felix,' dashing *in medias res*, rather than dallying over the matter. The author of 'The Old Arm Chair' makes use of many kinds of stationery, but her favourite emblem would seem to be a little dog over the motto *Credenda*. Of late years ill-health has compelled her to relinquish authorship.

Encore un poète! is the exclamation as the exquisitely beautiful manuscript of Monsieur Coppée meets our gaze. In all this collection it is the only specimen—save Gautier's—which recalls to mind the artistic and elaborate, yet fluent, calligraphy of our ancestry of the sixteenth and seventeenth centuries. Had it been a little more stately—a little less sparkling—it would have well passed for the workmanship of Montaigne or Bacon. Although the author of the 'Passant' may not rival the 'Good King Réné' in the manner of his initial-letters, nevertheless his capitals are superb, a fact well demonstrated by those of the *facsimile*. Solid, compact, and most picturesque is Coppée's chirography, and replete with all the quaint originalities appertaining to genius. The shape of the *sigma* in the Christian name is very characteristic of the whole style, which is sufficiently studied to need attention, but not so elaborate as to perplex the thoughtful. Artistic care has developed natural taste into the Beautiful, and created a form of handwriting anyone might pardonably be proud of.

Sir Michael Costa writes a fairly legible hand, but his
flourishes are most distressing : he flings them to and fro,
as if marking time with a *bâton*, instead of making notes
with a pen. Although by birth a Neapolitan, his writing
is somewhat French in appearance. His signature is not
so distinct as the rest of his epistle, and is endowed with
a tail, which, like those in popular periodicals, must be
'continued in our next,' for we cannot get the whole of
it into this page. He dates, but does not punctuate ;
he dots his 'i,' crosses his 't,' and makes his loops in
correct form. There is very little originality, and still
less beauty, about his calligraphy ; but it displays a
reasonable amount of care, and one would not hesitate
to assign an honourable post to its inditer as a reliable
man.

It is so long since the Burns centenary prize poem was won by a woman—moreover, the winner has since gone the way of most women, and been married—that her name is scarcely so familiar with the public as it might be. James Puckle, in that rare but exquisite little book of his, 'A Grey Cap for a Green Head,' says, ' A well-bred man will never give himself the liberty to speak ill of women ;' but this does not imply that he is not free to criticise their works. Isa Craig writes a somewhat masculine hand, and although her letters are fairly distinct, her calligraphy is more indicative of a public secretary or the manager of a public company than of a poetess. There is none of Eliza Cook's originality nor the feminine beauty of Christina Rossetti's handwriting in this style—little, in fact, to indicate the writer of probably the best, if not the only good, prize poem ever published in England. The unwieldy 'a' in the surname is an unusually poor letter for this lady, whose letters are generally fairly formed. With this exception, the autograph is better written than the rest of her manuscript, particularly the capitals, which, as a rule, are not her strong point. She does not punctuate, and frequently omits to cross the 't.' Her chirography is fairly bold and legible, but, as previously pointed out, is not very suggestive of the poet.

Darwin has certainly never carried out his idea of
'Natural Selection' in the choice of his letters, or he
would assuredly have managed to manufacture something
somewhat more legible than the scrawl he tries to palm
off upon his correspondents as writing. It is impossible
to criticise the form of his letters, as they are without form
and void, and, doubtless, of meaning to many. Job
stated that 'in the hands of all the sons of men' are
placed 'marks, that all the sons of men may know their
own works;' but really Darwin must be a better chiromancer than we are inclined to give him credit for, if he
can always decipher the marks of his own hand. Of such
hasty steel-penmanship, with many letters designated only
by a single stroke of his *stylus*, few would like to predicate a philosopher who, if he did not invent, at least
was the first to give form to the new scientific theory of
animal progression: few in these abortive 'pothooks and
hangers' would expect to find the patient investigator
and elaborate demonstrator. Darwin evidently under-
rates the importance of chirography, apparently deem-
ing it only a little valued means for the attainment of
an end. He often omits words, and then adds them
above a circumflex; he supplies the 'd' by a very rude
delta; puts the cross upon or above, but rarely across,
the 't;' abbreviates frequently; erases and alters occasionally; scarcely ever completes the formation of a letter,

and begins and ends his epistles as if in a terrible hurry. Most of his capitals are of the same form—if so it may be designated—as the smaller letters. He omits the year's date. His autograph is better done than most of his writing, from which, indeed, might be derived an idea of the immense labour that allows of no leisure, but not of the patient industry which leaves no fact unnoted likely to affect the truth of his proposition.

Certain physiologists, says Gautier, in the 'Grotesques,' assert that no one can be a great man who has not got a large nose, and the author of 'Le Nabob' would appear to deem a long tail necessary to the beauty of his *sigmas*: the size of the one is no more needed than the length of the other. The nasal apparatus of Socrates—whose greatness Monsieur Daudet will not question—was as flat as a flounder, and we have seen a far finer 's' than the French novelist ever achieved without any caudal appendage at all. Tails apart, Monsieur Daudet indites a neat, legible, and picturesque hand, characteristic of a moderately careful and well-gifted mind, with plenty of self-reliance, and not unmindful of making good use of the Present. His punctuation is forgetful, and his dating forgotten. It has been said that he who omits to date his letters does so for a purpose, but we should be sorry to impute any sinister motives to our author, verily believing that this omission *est sans rime ni raison*.

A certain family likeness runs through the calligraphy of many of the celebrated Confederates. As a rule they do not appear to have paid so much attention to handwriting as did some of their Northern opponents, but, politically, their signatures are clearer than those of most European statesmen. Jefferson Davis indites a fairly good style, somewhat too free, and scarcely shapely enough for our critical taste, but legible—as far as political legibility goes. Mr. Davis does not, or did not, punctuate, and his writing is not so typical of the highly educated man as is that of his Confederate associates—but then 'comparisons are odious,' and, in this case, doubtless deceptive. The manner of Mr. Davis is dictatorial, not to say, so far as our experience of his correspondence extends, tyrannical. The curtailment of the prænomen is curious.

'Oh! la belle chose que la Poste!' exclaims Sévigné in one of her charming letters, but then she was not referring to the expected arrival of a letter from Sir Charles. Truly, the author of 'Greater Britain' indites one of the worst hands in our collection, his signatures being, generally, even worse written than the body of the note, and varying continually in shape and wording. Amongst the various peculiarities observable in his chirography is the very eccentric one of beginning the personal pronoun 'he' with a capital letter. His short hurried notes—and he is rarely a voluminous correspondent in his own hand— are nearly illegible, and may have been inspired by that 'one of Brescia who,' according to old Pancirollus, 'published a way of writing which he thought impossible to be understood.' Like that *one*, Sir Charles's writing has also been 'unriddled and explained,' but he really might save his readers the trouble, for that he can do better when he likes, we know. Crippled, tortuous, and ill-formed, this handwriting, could its author not do better, would not inspire much belief in his talents. But he has much latent force in it, as in himself, and when he chooses can make it felt. The fact that the signature is generally poorer than the rest of his manuscript, would appear to hint at some amount of affectation in the wrong direction.

The handwriting of the Earl of Beaconsfield has changed its character as frequently as its author's fortunes have changed. Between the youthful enthusiast inditing a 'Revolutionary Epick' and a popular novelist defending Church and State in 'Lothair;' between a Radical candidate contesting Wycombe and Marylebone unsuccessfully, and a triumphant Tory Premier declining the people's wreath, the transition is not, perchance, greater than between the calligraphy of the one stage and that of another of Benjamin Disraeli's curious career. The writing of his mid-age is certainly more suggestive than that of his earlier or later years, but even then it varied from day to day. Generally, the hand may be described as bold and flashy; there is no trace of either the *littérateur* or the politician about it, and it changes its style

even more rapidly than the semi-fabulous chameleon its
hue. Sometimes an entire note has been decently written
—especially when intended to be complimentary in tone
—and upon other occasions scarcely a single letter has
been well formed, and only the autograph—upon which
extra carefulness is invariably lavished—has been present-
ably finished. So shifty and changeable a manner does
not inspire much confidence in the writer's stability of
purpose, although self-esteem may safely be predicated
from it.

The late Dr. Doran indited a somewhat effeminate old-fashioned hand, strangely reminiscent of good after-dinner anecdote and antique jest. The strokes are very shaky, and are inclined to indulge in a little self-satisfactory flourish—needless, but not unsuited to nor uncharacteristic of the whole style. The small letters have no originality and little variety, the c, e, and i are all alike, their respective powers having to be gathered from the context. As with most *literati*, his final 'd' takes the shape of the Greek *delta*, but Dr. Doran's is a very poor specimen. His signature is rather larger, and much better built, than the body of his manuscript, and is evidently very carefully constructed; the 'r' in it is differently formed from his usual way of writing that letter. No originality nor vigour could be predicated from such *Handschrift*, but pleasant gossip and story might readily be anticipated from its inditer.

Monsieur Doré has read Shakespeare, or at the worst his *traduction*, and may therefore be reminded that he says, ' *Your* date is better in a pie or pudding than in *your* letter ; ' for what help is it to us that he heads his notes *Mercredi*, or any other day, an' he omit the month and year? At first glance, indeed, the *tout-ensemble* of 'Golden' Gustave's calligraphy is not very reassuring, a page of it looking more like a *bouquet de crotte* than anything else we can think of. But it improves somewhat upon inspection, and assumes a dramatic, or rather melo-dramatic air, very suggestive of stage effect, the words gradually growing legible, although their constituent parts are in a very chaotic condition. Generally the initial letter of the word, or syllable, is pretty clearly written, then the succeeding 'pothooks and hangers' begin to deteriorate in value, growing small by degrees, and anything but beautifully less, until the unfortunate final, if it be born at all, is nothing but an abortive little dot or dash. The separate letters are scarcely worth criticising, they are so meagre and hastily scrawled. The signature is larger and far better shaped than the rest of Monsieur Doré's writing, the general impression given of which is rather suggestive of scene-painting than anything more artistic, although it is easy to discern that its author could indite a far better hand did he care to.

The author of 'Monte Christo'—probably the most popular romance of modernity—indited a meretricious hand, full of flourish, but clearer and with better formed letters than many of his *confrères* made. He did not always *mettre le point sur les i*, nor did he deem it necessary to cross his 't;' but for these little deficiencies he compensated his correspondents with coils of twist and twirl that environed his alphabet with Laokoön-like convolutions. Sometimes he punctuated, and sometimes he did not. His handwriting grew shaky towards the end of his story, but it always maintained its resemblance, in many noteworthy respects, to his earlier mannerisms, as, for instance, in occasional intensely thick black down strokes, alternating with fine hair lines. Such samples of calligraphy are by no means scarce, and indicate a good knowledge of effect without any symptoms of genius; no imagination to originate, but plenty of skill at superficial combination, and often a capital eye for local colour. No legitimate member of the *genus irritabile vatum* ever wrote such a conventionally disposed hand as did the elder Dumas, but many feuilletonists have; not, indeed, that many folks of the latter class equal the author of 'Les Trois Mousquetaires' in brilliancy of composition or charm of workmanship.

The author of 'L'Étrangère' has had the fortune of having a father born before him, and inherited a famous name if nothing else. Generally, probably from his fondness for antithesis, his calligraphy is as devoid of decoration as his father's was florid : the only flourish he permits himself is an enormous tail to the loop of the 'f' of the *fils*. Beyond this rare cuticular ornament—*et c'est le plus difficile que d'écorcher la queue*—he most carefully eschews all the examples of whirlwindy embellishment set by Dumas *père*. In one respect his writing resembles that of the first Alexandre, it is generally legible : it is heavy, black, and forcible, but with a tendency to suppress the final letters of a word. As with many other writers who form their letters with so much determination, the different syllables of a word are often left unconnected. Although he did write such twaddle as 'La Dame aux Camélias'—once upon a time deemed an immoral book—Dumas the Second's hand is indicative of a higher order of talent than his father's : it is typical of greater stability and power.

Emily Faithfull's handwriting is one of the semi-masculine styles: occasionally it reminds one of Eliza Cook's, but is not nearly so vigorous, is more variable, and less characteristic than the poet's. Miss Faithfull writes backwards, and as if in a terrible hurry, but her letters lean in every direction at once, whilst the lines sway up and down, as if afflicted with vertigo. Her calligraphy is not good; at times, indeed, is barely readable, and the chirographist would be disposed to deem it rather more characteristic of hard work than originality—more indicative of ability to labour than power to invent. Editorial duties, however, have probably modified, and rendered difficult to decipher with certainty, the chirographical mysteries of this writing. The autograph is a good specimen of Miss Faithfull's manuscript, and it is not too legible. We have already referred to the remark of the poet Rogers, that he who wrote his name obscurely was guilty of a piece of impertinence to the person addressed; but that, of course, only applies to the unfair sex, man's better half having *carte blanche* for any and every thing.

A scratchy handwriting, neither attractive nor legible, was that of Sir William Fergusson. His signature, however, used to be so much better executed than the general text of his epistles, that it is impossible to believe him not capable of doing better had he pleased. A man whose moments were so precious might be forgiven that his letters looked as if hastily written, but why need Sir William have wasted so much time over those spiteful-looking and utterly needless complications of flourishes? As a rule his smaller letters were badly formed, and some of his capitals were not readable. No medical prescription, and that is saying a good deal, could be more illegible than his usual calligraphy. Sir William dated, but did not punctuate. His autographic flourish it has been found necessary to curtail.

Edward A Freeman

Those who write history are generally more careful than those who make it. Mr. Freeman, however, does not appear to exercise such care in the selection of his stylus as does the present Ameer of Afghanistan, Yacoob, who, when signing the bran new treaty with Great Britain, rejected the reeds proffered him, and cut one for himself, remarking, 'It is always best for a man to make his own pen when he has anything particular to write.' Whether the Ameer's penmanship will endure as long as the historian's is beside the question. Mr. Freeman's manuscript, however, is nearer what Southey styled 'uglyography' than calligraphy; his letters are unshapely and not too legible; his vowels are rarely looped; some letters rise far above their lineal limits, and many are ununiform in slope. Punctuation is ignored; 'i' left undotted; 't' occasionally uncrossed, and many sad evidences of haste are left about the page. This is not what one would expect in the manuscript of him who is to teach the Present by telling the truth about the Past. Correct dating, careful signature, and the virile *tout-ensemble* of the whole style, however, proclaim a man who has something noteworthy to say, even if he does not say it in his best manner.

'Ah, Freedom is a noble thing!' sang old Barbour, but we do not think because a man is a good patriot he is entitled to take liberties with his *Handschrift* such, *zu Beispiel*, as the late Herr Ferdinand Freiligrath did with his autograph. The last shall be first in this instance, as, veritably, it is the worst word of his manuscript, and quite undecipherable, save to experts. The rest of the patriot-poet's chirography is legibly although too hastily indited. The various members of his alphabet are elegantly formed but have no virility; they are emasculate, *petite*, and slight, and do not suggest any manliness. They are fairly free from flourish, and—as does, also, the imperfectly constructed signature—appear to proffer the idea of a man somewhat deficient in self-esteem.

When Cincinnatus returned to his plough he probably paid more attention to turning his furrows neatly than to cultivating the elegancies of calligraphy. Now-a-days retired patriots are not permitted to enjoy their *otium cum dignitate* apart from the outer world's ken, and Garibaldi—no more than any other distinguished individual—is not allowed to flourish unheard even if unseen. His truest friends, indeed, deem it a pity that the old general does indulge in his chirographical exploits, but with that we have nothing to do: our duty is to judge the form and fashion of his letters' constituent parts. A clear, straightforward, unvarnished style is that indited by the far-famed Italian, unmarked by any particular mannerisms or eccentricities, and not very unlike an English hand in its most salient features. The autograph is, in every respect, representative.

Gautier's calligraphy is one of the most singular to be met with. As a rule his writing was most exquisitely fine, smaller and more delicate than De Banville's, and often as beautiful and legible as that of Edgar Poe—the supreme prince of manuscript. At other times his handwriting was larger, and more closely resembled that of our sixteenth century ancestors than that of any author's we are acquainted with. It was always beautiful and most original. His autograph is scarcely so *recherché* as the usual run of his correspondence, the initial letter in the surname being more than ordinarily *bizarre*, although well adapted to the natural style of the author of 'Les Grotesques.' It is scarcely to be wished that so minute a mode of chirography will ever become common, but its legibility and originality are deserving all praise. The author of such a hand could never, by any possible chance, be an ordinary person.

[Signature: W. E. Gladstone]

Previous to the introduction of post-cards, this Right Honourable gentleman indited a clear, undemonstrative, and readable hand of the usual parliamentary type. It was scarcely so bold as Mr. Bright's nor so picturesque as Cobden's: was not so 'flashy' as (the then) Mr. Disraeli's, and was more straightforward than Mr. Roebuck's. The chief defect was the uncertainty. Some of the letters, more particularly the capitals, were really elegant specimens of calligraphy, but the hand could not be relied on. After a few remarkably well-formed words would follow a regiment of far inferior-shaped alphabetical militia, suffering from the many defects to which ill-drilled men are liable; whilst the halt, the maimed, and the deformed were all there represented, too numerously for separate recapitulation. Since the postal innovation above alluded to, the Right Honourable's chirography has fallen into chaos. Our *facsimile* is, of course, from a signature prior to that lamentable descent.

Sit tibi terra levis, thou talented son of misfortune! The gods forbid that our pen should press heavily upon aught that remains of poor Albert Glatigny, the descendant of Villon, the godson of *les maîtres* Victor Hugo, De Banville, and, perhaps, Baudelaire. The hero of that saddest of all *Jours de l'An* known did not indite a writing-master's copper-plate, but, for all that, his calligraphy was a clear, original, and fluent one. The somewhat florid, and somewhat extravagant autograph, was not out of keeping with the man, although much larger, at least as far as the capitals were concerned, than the generality of his manuscript, and is not unsuggestive of his frequent attempts to *prendre la lune avec les dents*, as his witty compatriots say. Many of his epistles were written under such difficulties that they could scarcely be accepted as full specimens of his powers; nevertheless, they are all fully suggestive of the poor young poet so sympathetically described by him who chooses to be known as M. Job Lazare. Chirographical eccentricities proper to Glatigny are suppression of the curved upstrokes in certain consonants, disconnection of many letters which should be joined, and similar little *fantaisies de poète*.

The calligraphy of the author of 'On Viol and Flute' has wonderfully improved during the last few years, and is really very charming in tone, although somewhat too *petite* for legibility. Mr. Gosse makes some very pretty capitals, but occasionally, and, perchance, designedly, they are only the small letters of the alphabet 'writ large.' In fact he has, apparently, a *penchant* for small forms, although not so bad as that Peter Bale who is recorded to have written the Lord's Prayer, the Creed, the Ten Commandments, two Latin prayers, and what else only the gods know, in the compass of a silver penny! Mr. Gosse must be credited with the manufacture of several delightful curls and curves in connection with his letters, but at times he invents purely arbitrary forms: for instance, curiously shaped 'ss,' do duty for 'gs,' and other chirographical freaks of fancy bedeck his manuscript. He carefully eschews flourish; makes his signature considerably larger than the rest of the writing; and, all in all, indites a hand which, if not very original nor very vigorous, is characteristically graceful.

The author of the 'Faust' music writes a very pretty little French hand, which, need it be said, is a very different thing from an English one. His epistles are clear, neat, and characteristic, with but few erasures or alterations. His letters are small, yet must be a relief to readers after the scrawls which too many of his countrymen indulge in. Unfortunately, however, he sometimes writes with blue ink upon blue paper, which gives one the blues to peruse. His most prominent trait is a seeming inability to form capitals different from the small letters in anything save size. He is more attentive to punctuation than the generality of his *confrères*, but occasionally his accents and commas attain monstrous proportions, whilst at intervals he cannot refrain from such wild flourishes as the autograph affords a specimen of. Undoubtedly the idiosyncrasies of M. Gounod are varied and strongly marked. Finicalness, eccentricity, and a certain amount of self-satisfaction, might safely be predicated of this scribe.

The handwriting of the late ex-minister is not a very handsome one, and should be relegated to that mediocre class which includes within its narrow limits the busy trader and the still busier politician—the two parallel professions which live upon the wants of the general public, and persuade that public that they only labour *pro bono publico*. Monsieur Guizot's is a small, fretful, but fairly legible hand, offering little or no trace of literary occupation. There are few marked peculiarities about it, the most decided being the occasional curious form of the 'i,' the dot of which is equal in size to the entire letter, which letter is, indeed, only a second dot. Nothing very pleasing could be predicated from this style, and as, *de mortuis nil nisi verum*, we are silent, leaving the autograph to speak for us.

Andrew Halliday's calligraphy was a very singular and picturesque one, and more legible than casual readers might imagine. He did not fritter away his labour over preposterous flourishes, but he did depreciate the value of his penmanship by annoying contractions, and by the careless way in which he crossed his 't' and dotted his 'i,' these finishing touches being deposited at random at any distance from their proper letters. His punctuation, like that of his *confrères*, was conspicuous by its absence. His autograph is somewhat larger than his ordinary writing, which is *petite*, and is distinguished from the general hand by having capitals, his usual plan having been to furnish somewhat enlarged copies of the small letters. All faults noted, it is impossible not to like Mr. Halliday's *Handschrift*. It is literary looking, characteristic of energy and *esprit*, and indicates a careful and foreseeing scribe. Although he may not have been willing to adopt the precept of Horace, *Nonumque prematur in annum*, he was not likely, in our chirographical opinion, to spoil a good thing by too much haste.

The Vestal Virgins could not have devoted more care to the preservation of the Sacred Fire, than Mr. Bret Harte must exercise over his microscopically minute calligraphy, in order to maintain its legibility. In fact, despite the real beauty of his handwriting, our Californian friend has drawn down his 'pothooks and hangers' to such Lilliputian dimensions, that he may be considered to have brought them to a *reductio ad absurdum*. In chirography, as in all things, a happy medium may be preserved, and whilst Polyphemian proportions should be avoided on the one hand, on the other, Aristratosian[1] invisibility is equally undesirable. Certainly it must be conceded that Bret Harte's handwriting, however diminutive, is clearly, and generally correctly, shaped. A fondness for looping two or three words together, and the occasional suppression of a letter, are the chief faults—beyond the smallness—calling for animadversion. Seen through a microscope, the calligraphy is a fairly commendable one, and proves its author to be a careful and painstaking man. A spice of quaintness would have improved its character :—

Which the same I am free to maintain.

---

[1] Aristratos was so small that he was said to be invisible.

Hervé indites a most terrifying style, with scrolls and flourishes flashing half across the page. Wild, scratchy, and fantastic looking as are his epistles, strange to say, they possess a qualification not too common with the productions of French composers: they are quite legible. This may be partially attributed to the fact that the author of 'Chilperic' makes his 'pothooks and hangers' of a larger size than is usual with his countrymen, and partially to the fact that, with all his braggadocio-looking air, one readily perceives that M. Hervé strives to be intelligible. The quaintness of his calligraphy is not of beauty but of exaggeration. He dots the 'i' and sometimes crosses the 't,' does his best at punctuation, and altogether affords the idea of a man assuming a carelessness and extravagance which are not native to him; and it is easy to perceive that the composer of 'Le Petit Faust' —a very good thing in its *petit* way—only puts on the cap and bells for a purpose.

The writing of no American poet is so pleasing to us as that of Oliver Wendell Holmes. It is somewhat old-fashioned, like his verse, and like that has the polish of a man accustomed to good society; is, indeed, that of a gentleman. There are no needless flourishes on the one hand, nor unsightly contractions on the other, but there is a very determined kind of finish to nearly every word, as much as to say, 'I am Dr. Holmes, and Dr. Holmes, as you are aware, is somebody.' There is just that amount of independence to be looked for in this writer as would preserve him from doing a shabby act, without any trace of those flourishes which betoken offensive egotism. A fluent, clear, gracefully quaint chirography is that of the 'Professor,' with just enough dash about it to intimate the humour for which Holmes—the witty wise—is famous. The tails of letters carried below the line do not loop, but have a merry twirl, apparently suggestive of their writer's drolleries. If we have any fault to find with Holmes's *Handschrift*, it is that, as a rule, it is written with too fine a quill. His signature has greatly improved of late, and is better executed than the body of his letters. It is impossible that a man who writes as the 'Professor' does could be anything but kind-hearted.

R. H. Horne

Some persons have the misfortune to be born before their time, but posterity endeavours to rectify the mistake by erecting statues of them and mentioning their virtues in encyclopædias. Mr. Horne is more unfortunate than those men; he was born *after* his time, and ancestry cannot help him. Had he written his grand dramas in the days of Elizabeth, or his great epic 'Orion' in the time of the Commonwealth, he would now be classed among our *Dii majorum gentium*. As it is, he is chiefly known to those who know and love choice poetry, and their name, it is to be feared, is not legion. His calligraphy has been somewhat modified by circumstances, but it is still as firm and decided as if its writer, instead of being seventy-three, were only thirty-seven. Such handwriting—noble, clear, and picturesque—betokens in the most unequivocal manner the leading characteristics of his massive intellect. The signature scarcely conveys the general style of his composition so well as the body of his letters.

The signature of Victor Hugo, as that of, *par excellence*, the foremost poet, patriot, orator, and representative of France in the nineteenth century, will, presumedly, have as much, if not more, interest for the greatest number as any in this *répertoire*. For many years the calligraphy of *le maître des maîtres* has but slightly varied from the type it assumed in early manhood, although from time to time his autograph has altered, not in form, but in formula. Even the vacillations of genius are noteworthy, therefore it is not uninteresting to study the variations which have taken place in the signature of 'Hernani's' author. Under the Restoration it was 'V⁰ʳ M. Hugo,' later the second initial was dropped, and then, after another lapse of time, the signature became 'V. Hugo,' eventually changing to 'Victor Hugo,' in which last form it has remained for thirty or more years unchanged, save when subscribed to intimate friends, in which case it is simply 'Victor,' or initials. The autograph given above is a better specimen of the poet's style than can often be obtained, especially as regards the first capital, a letter Victor Hugo frequently writes in a more pointed or angular manner. His general chirography, though frequently indited in an extremely hasty way, is tolerably legible and fairly picturesque, and does not, as may be well imagined, offer the slightest traits of the conventional. The chief peculiarity, and one that imparts considerable brilliancy to his manuscript, is the original formation of the small 'v,' which is generally larger than the other letters, and looped like the capital 'V' of the signature. The accents are frequently neglected, the punctuation defective, and the formation of many of the letters incomplete. No one, however, could glance over this chirography without arriving at the conclusion that it was the production of an illustrious personage.

Our professors affect a metal *stylus*, and are mostly bad writers. Now-a-days, Professor Huxley, who did write fairly well in former times, seems to have less leisure, and even a worse pen, than his *confrères*. Not

The assessor's pen,
Recording answers shriek'd upon the rack,

could express itself in more tortured letters than does Huxley's. When it has been stated that all his strokes slope one way, all the good that can be said of his writing has been said. The renowned physiologist omits to punctuate, and he might just as well omit to date, his letters, for his figures are perfectly illegible. The autograph is no worse, is, indeed, not so bad as the body of his letters. To predicate anything from such scrawls would be impossible : there is not a single letter in the professor's calligraphy deserving our commendation.

The good folks of Zocotra were Christians and, says an ancient writer, 'les plus honnêtes gens du monde, sans autre défaut que celui de n'entendre rien dans la religion qu'ils professent.' Father Ignatius appears to be in a similar condition of blissful ignorance, so far, at least, as regards calligraphy, for the scrawl he palms off as handwriting is little more than a few higgledy-piggledy pothooks and hangers having a scramble over the paper. This scribble, made by a pen, stick, or other handy implement, is like 'the tale told by an idiot,' and, so far as our chirographical insight is concerned, must be held as 'signifying nothing.'

There hath been many a General Jackson, but only one 'Stonewall' so hight, and his calligraphy is thoroughly characteristic of that man. There is some faint resemblance in the letters to those of General Lee, partly because our specimens of both were indited by steel pens—those villanous suppressors of natural traits—and partly by the exigence of active service. 'Stonewall' Jackson's hand is the better of the two, being less stiff, and the letters of it more shapely in form. His military minutes are of the most laconic style possible, not a single word, or letter, or even stroke being superfluous. He was inclined to hurry the final letters of his words and to vary the forms of his capitals. A somewhat feminine cast in his writing would suggest the belief that the man who faced bullets more composedly than many do snowflakes, was of a gentle, even soft-hearted nature. The autograph is somewhat less pronounced than the general manuscript, the impression left by which is one of a retiring and kindly, albeit firm disposition, without any trace of the dashing trooper.

The calligraphy of this Confederate Cato—*Victrix causa Diis placuit, sed victa Catoni*—is more idiosyncratic than that of his compeers, albeit it is not free from their fault of school-boyish hair-strokes, a fault destructive of individuality. It is a small, neatly-made, and somewhat feminine, but by no means effeminate, style of writing. All the letters are clearly but not very correctly shaped, and their slope is extremely variable. His composition, an art too closely connected with the philosophy of handwriting to be neglected in its study, is terse, suggestive, and occasionally antithetic in tone. Among his minor divergences from the rules of handwriting proper may be noted a disposition to ignore the lower loops of the small letters—his capitals are all looped—and a great want of uniformity in the heights and depths of the different pothooks and hangers. The signature is somewhat more uniform, and consequently less representative than the body of General Johnston's writing, the whole of which has evidently been modified by extraneous circumstances, although it might safely be predicated to be that of a farsighted if not remarkable man.

Although probably more popular from his labours in other ways of life, it is our belief that as the author of a few priceless lyrics Charles Kingsley's fame will be most durable, and as a poet we would judge his deeds. Unlike the common run of university men, his handwriting shows traces of the elements of beauty, but excessive work has deteriorated its quality. A variety of pressing duties have left their signs of haste on Kingsley's calligraphy, and give to his letters the appearance of flourishes—from which vulgarity, however, they are free. His chief definite fault is the making his 'm' and 'n' like a string of 'ees:' this defect is even apparent in the autograph. A manly, earnest hand, thoroughly characteristic of the Chartist clergyman, has been spoilt by too much work and 'too many irons in the fire.'

A manly and somewhat military style characterises the autograph of the famous Hungarian patriot, although it wavers in an uncertain manner between the Latin and German letters in form. Of this halting between the two characters—by no means unusual, so far as Hungarian calligraphy is concerned—the signature is a very fair specimen, affording as it does in nearly every letter traces of Teutonic influence. The flourish is not a very elegant one, but is a very favourite decoration with foreign commanders. It would require a larger quantity of his manuscript than we have yet examined to lay down any very positive laws with respect to this writer's personal traits, but no one can inspect even his autograph without deciding that it is the calligraphy of a supremely honourable even if somewhat self-willed man: not a stroke but proclaims its maker's independence of thought.

Valentine's magnificent white marble recumbent figure of Lee,

> Like a warrior taking his rest,
> With his martial cloak around him,

is, probably, one of the most successful, because most natural, statues of this century. The chisel of the talented Virginian sculptor recalls the face and form of the famous Confederate general for those who can visit his beautiful mausoleum at Lexington, but those who cannot must be contented to view his calligraphy. General Robert E. Lee's writing was of an old-fashioned somewhat formal school, such, doubtless, as Colonel Newcome indited, and without being elegant was aristocratic. It was fairly legible, determined and dark in the down strokes, but too thin and hair-like in the up lines. The first half of the 'w' was generally an 'e,' whilst many other minor defects are apparent in it. The style is very unliterary, and is chiefly suggestive of staunch integrity and strong determination.

Few folks appear to be aware that of the one thousand and one *littérateurs* who have essayed the impossible task of transmuting into English equivalents the mingled pathos and humour of Heine's poesy, the genial 'Hans Breitmann' has been nearest the goal. And in calligraphy, few of his countrymen have so nearly reached our ideas of excellence. Not, indeed, that Mr. Leland's hand is free from fault, but we, like Suetonius with the Cæsars, elect to mention virtues as well as vices, when we get the chance. The author of the 'Breitmann Ballads' indites a style pleasant to look on, and, but for its tendency to flourish, of a poetic, quaint form : a style replete with scriptory *chiaro-oscuro*, and very suggestive of originality and imagination. A little more compression, less dash, and a greater regard for the minor technicalities of our science, and we should have awarded a very high position among our calligraphical candidates to Charles G. Leland.

If the man who causes an extra blade of grass to spring up is deserving of gratitude, what does not Count de Lesseps deserve, who has brought the Eastern world many days' distance nearer to the Western. All honour to him and the country which aided him. We have not yet heard, however, that the empire which has most benefited by his scheme has overwhelmed the great engineer with marks of its gratitude. Probably it is saving up a portion of the profits accruing to the nation from the Suez Canal for a marble monument to its constructor when he dies. As regards the calligraphy of Ferdinand de Lesseps, nothing very striking in it calls for notice : it is a free, fluent, clear, and somewhat feminine style, but without any very marked traits. Neither imagination nor study are displayed very strongly in the Count's calligraphy; it is, indeed, somewhat more suggestive of the skilful financier than of the inventive genius.

With all due admiration for Jenny Lind's vocal accomplishments, her chirographical efforts, it must be confessed, do not earn our approbation. She would never rival the famous St. Theckla—who wrote out the entire Scriptures without blur or blot—for mistakes and alterations are of no infrequent occurrence in the modern lady's epistles. Her autograph is far superior to the general body of her manuscript, the chirography of which is by no means legible, at any rate when written in English, in which language Madame Goldschmidt is, of course, labouring under disadvantage. That her handwriting is too large does not so much matter—as there was no real necessity to get the Iliad into a nutshell—but the absence of form about nearly every letter is most inartistic and quite distressing. Some of this lady's words dash almost across the page, whilst others shoot forth wonderful extraneous limbs that attempt to perform equally marvellous acrobatic feats. Madame Goldschmidt sometimes writes on one side only of the paper, she utterly ignores punctuation, and, in fact, produces such a wild sort of calligraphy that having much of it to decipher would exhaust the patience of the most Joblike of experts.

The author of 'Joshua Davidson' indites one of the best—if not the best—hands in this collection appertaining to literary ladies. Although by no means free from fault, it is a neat, vigorous, and *compressed* style, very noticeable, as regards this last quality, as emanating from the better half of humanity. Women when writing a fluent hand generally degenerate into ultra dashiness, the result of which may appear brilliant, but is not typical of real strength. There is, indeed, a restrained power about Mrs. Lynn Lynton's calligraphy strongly indicative of individuality. The concentrated force and *chic* of her style is anything but suggestive of *cathedræ molles*. Her capitals are her best letters. Having said thus much on behalf of this lady's writing, it must now be confessed that, in many respects, it is far from perfect. Its author often runs two or more words into one by a series of lateral bands; sometimes she suppresses the last and even the penultimate letters of a word; her 'n' is made similar in shape to the 'u;' she rarely dots her 'i,' and, in fact, commits various chirographical *faux pas*. The autograph is better than the rest of her manuscript, the whole of which is suggestive of something more than mere study.

If the gods were authors they might be expected to indite a style not very dissimilar from Leconte de Lisle's. In this collection there is not a more virile, vigorous, and grandiose hand than that of the French poet: each letter in it is a veritable *tour de force*. Capitals, and the minor members of his alphabetical family, are equally noble, equally legible, and all picturesque. The slight tendency to flourish is restrained by an iron will, and the impulse is expended in a determined but terse termination to the last letter of each word, save only in the thoroughly idiosyncratic signature. The uniformity in size and slope of the characters is most artistic, whilst the variety and originality of their forms forbid the faintest suspicion of sameness. Pindar might have been proud to write his Dithyrambs with Leconte de Lisle's stylus, so splendid and stately is the calligraphy which flows from it. It is not possible to imagine that anything trivial could sully the grandeur of such an Olympian style, and it would ill become us to seek if petty faults be hidden in these magnificent characters—which should be regarded as sacred as the daughters of Jove.

Cotton's translation, or rather paraphrase of Horace,

> He must sharp cold and scorching heat despise,
> And most tempt danger where most danger lies,

seems to predicate the chief characteristics of the late David Livingstone. Of course a man accustomed to daily defy death in African wilds, and to spend his hours in traversing, amid countless dangers, the weirdest lands and most savage hordes of men, could scarcely be expected to practise the most elegant calligraphy. All things considered, however, the famous traveller's handwriting is by no means despicable: there is a statuesque, grand simplicity about it very attractive, although many of the technicalities of handwriting are ignored, and the formation of several letters is anything but exact. The 'a' is made generally like 'e' followed by an 'i,' and the 'g' of a similar style of manufacture—like 'e' followed by 'j.' These, and other kindred peculiarities, are the result of endeavouring to write all the letters of a word without removing the pen from the paper. The chirography is rather too large, as will be seen by the thoroughly characteristic autograph, but is very indicative of a manly and reliable disposition.

As evidence of how contradictory men's actions are, so that it seems impossible they should proceed from one and the same person, Montaigne alludes to the instance of 'Nero, the perfect image of all cruelty, when having the sentence of a condemned man brought to him to sign, cried out, "Oh, that I had never been taught to write!"' Without wishing to compare the kindly author of 'London Lyrics' to the blood-bathed Cæsar, we deem the excerpt *apropos* of his calligraphical styles —for he has several. Sometimes Mr. Frederick Locker indites a hasty, scratchy, and by no means too legible a hand; at another time he writes in a fine, *petite*, perfectly clear mode, but with several abbreviations; whilst, thirdly, he favours his correspondents with a firm, compact, and picturesque style, such as is shown by the autograph. The signature, and, by the way, its writer frequently subscribes himself as 'F. L.' only, is very characteristic of the style last mentioned. As so often happens in the body of his manuscript, one letter is seen sloping backwards, as if recoiling from its partner. In this last style every letter is clearly and happily formed, not a flourish is introduced nor a limb amputated, the punctuation is perfect, and every requisite of letter-writing—save always the year's date—is supplied. This singular fluctuation of styles, this transition 'from grave to gay, from lively to severe,' is, probably, truly typical of the writer of our *vers de société*, symbolizing the change from wit to pathos so well pleaded for in 'The Jester's Plea.'

Certainly Longfellow is the most popular of his country's bards, even if he be not, as claimed by Edgar Poe, 'entitled to the first place among the poets of America.' His calligraphy is not much to our taste, whatever may be thought of his poetry : it is unpleasing that it is written backwards, and because of its evident artificiality. The capital 'W' in the autograph has but to be investigated in order to render these remarks fully comprehensible. The flourish to the capital 'L' is very unsightly, and would appear to be a modern innovation, as it is not noticeable in some of its author's earlier signatures, nor is it, indeed, always so exaggerated as in the above specimen. The 'H' is simply preposterous for a man of genius—which the author of 'Hiawatha' undoubtedly is. The smaller letters of Longfellow's chirography are more commendable; they have no affected flourishes, and, although too large, are fairly proportionate with one another in size. As a rule, the lines are equidistant, and in some cases, apparently, have been guided by marked lines. The upper loops of the letters are much too large, whilst where the lower loops should be they are utterly ignored. This poet's writing so far follows the rudimentary requirements of our art as to be extremely readable, and shows that he has a horror of being misunderstood; indeed, he even condescends —*rara avis* amid the swans of Helicon!—to scratch out *errata* with a *knife!* But there is little natural fluency about this script: it is sicklied o'er with the pale cast of thought, and is a manufactured style more significant of the length of Art than the fleetness of Time.

J. R. Lowell.

The handwriting of James Russell Lowell is far more sightly than that of his *confrère* Longfellow, and would prognosticate greater wealth of imagination and more terseness of style than its author has yet given evidence of. Everything about this chirography indicates the man of artistic perception and completeness. No vainglorious flourish nor affected strainings after originality disfigure this autograph, which is severely simple, yet graceful, and just what one would wish a poet's to be. Writing, of course, to some extent differs in accordance with difference of the pen it flows from, but it seems to us that, even after allowing for this cause, Lowell's script is not quite so massive as it was in former years. Certainly his signature is thinner, and the few peculiarities it possesses, such as the final 'd' being something between the German and the Greek form of that letter, and the tail of the 'y' being turned backwards, are more pronounced than of yore. Of his humour,—and although that may be the best of its kind, *that kind* of verse should never be desecrated by the name of Poetry—His Excellency's calligraphy gives no intimation, unless the somewhat spiteful-looking cross to his 't,' which strongly resembles Carlyle's, may be deemed indicative of it. His epistles would afford good 'copy' to the printer, being clearly written, punctuated, and paragraphed.

Sir John Lubbock might, could, and should write a good style, but his multifarious occupations have been too much for him: haste has deteriorated what would otherwise have been a noble hand. Without some clue —*sans le mot d'enigme*—not the most acute of experts could decipher the last syllable of his name—the 'bock' might baffle the most cunning of chirographists. *Festina lente* would be the best advice for such rapid writers. A tendency to spoil many good schemes by attempting too much at once might be feared of the writer of this autograph, but at the same time, manliness, vigorous and shrewd good sense might safely be ascribed to him. 'The long result of Time' should certainly not be despised by the author of 'Prehistoric Man.' The capital 'J' of his signature is not without force, but it is a force misapplied; the head is too hydrocephalus-looking for so diminutive a tail. Many of his twists it would be a misnomer to call letters, and the capital 'L' is the only really good representative of the alphabet, and it, it should be acknowledged, is very elegant.

The present owner of Knebworth writes in a style very similar in many respects to that indited by Wilkie Collins, but, as a rule, it must be averred that the former is the better chirographist of the two, even in his most hurried notes. Although Lord Lytton rarely dots his 'i' or crosses his 't,' his letters are better built and more compact than are those of the famous novelist, whilst their extra grace and quaintness are more indicative of a poetic imagination. Some of the *soi disant* 'Owen Meredith's' calligraphy of a few years back is very beautiful, and, despite pressure of viceregal duties, and the chilling effect of high office, the hand still retains its wonted cunning. His vowels are nearly always as handsome as legible, and without the slightest intimation of that *banal* air which so frequently accompanies the distinct writing of commonplace people. The punctuation is good, but abbreviations occasionally occur, such as the substitution of '&' for 'and'—and the initial letters of words, especially when they are 'ys,' are apt to begin backwards. A noble, hearty, and richly imaginative mind—somewhat constrained by pressure of office—might be predicated from such calligraphy, the autograph of which is thoroughly representative.

Belles lettres would be a very fair appellation for Mr. McCarthy's 'pothooks and hangers.' Although by no means perfect as a specimen of handwriting, no one can deny to this elegant and picturesque calligraphy a due meed of praise. Despite the beauty of such chirography, enough fault can be found with it to prevent this page becoming little more than a note of admiration! That many of his letters have to go without loops may be attributed to the pressure upon his time now-a-days, Mr. McCarthy having forsaken his former wise abstention from practical politics, and added to his labour of writing the 'History of Our Own Times' that of assisting in the manufacture of the history itself. Many of his letters have just the slightest approach to a flourish, a merry little twinkle about their tops and tails that gives them a most insinuating look, not altogether unsuggestive of the renowned stone which this gentleman's (presumed) ancestor, King Cormack MacCarthy, caused to be suitably inscribed some four or more centuries ago. An original, but somewhat puzzling air, is given to this manuscript by the *outré* way in which the up and down strokes vary in thickness. It is a still stronger excess of this same peculiarity that gives so quaint a tone to Mr. Tennyson's calligraphy. There is more of the poet than the politician, indeed, exhibited in Mr. McCarthy's chirography, and still more humorous good-nature than either those classes of beings are generally accredited with the possession of.

Stéphane Mallarmé

Had we premiums to award for beautiful calligraphy, the author of 'L'après-midi d'un Faune' would certainly obtain the grand prize. However hastily indited, the calligraphy of Stéphane Mallarmé is invariably elegant: it looks so fluent that the inexpert may deem it carelessly done—*insouciant comme un papillon*—but, if so, it is far more graceful than the most careful composition of his *confrères*. It does not possess the grandeur of Leconte de Lisle's, nor the *riante fantaisie* of de Banville's chirography, but in harmony and beauty is unsurpassed by any. The characters, though small, are clear, and without the faintest approach to a flourish are finished off to the ultimate curve or curl. Every calligraphical detail is complete, from the *alpha* of the date to the *omega* of the superscription, and all this, including scrupulous punctuation, without an iota of schoolcraft or clerkly formality. Replete with graceful strokes of fancy, Mallarmé's calligraphy fully realises Victor Hugo's line, 'Ton beau style, étoilé de fraîches métaphores,' and seems, every line of it, to exhale the dainty aroma of Poesy! It may be truly said that it is *munus Appoline dignum!*

W. H. Mallock.

Is Calligraphy deserving an Author's notice, is no impertinent question to put the author of 'Is Life worth Living?' At any rate, it is to be hoped that when 'The New Republic' gets beyond an after-dinner symposium Mr. Mallock will not be appointed Minister of Instruction—unless he improve his penmanship. His writing is utterly devoid of beauty, and, save in the affectation of the signature, almost exempt from originality. It is unpleasant to have to cauterise so severely, but it is necessary in a case like this, when the invalid's cure is dependent upon himself. Mr. Mallock, unlike some less favoured deipnosophists, has only to discard his little affectations, and devote care to his calligraphy, to become a master of our art. At present, his letters are all up and down the page, like an awkward squad, and scarcely one is correctly built: a single stroke—and that not too straight—is frequently made to do duty for an elaborate alphabetical symbol. Not a favourable word may be said for any of his letters; from *alpha* to *omega*, they are all more or less suffering under malformation. The signature is far better than the other portions of Mr. Mallock's manuscript.

Manet's script is the very opposite of the ordinary Parisian's, and is, indeed, somewhat English in style. The great 'Impressionist' handles his pen as if he disdained the aid of so slight an implement, dashing out his letters in furious fashion. There is no hesitation—no courtly grace—about this calligraphy, which is, indeed, far more suggestive of a Rembrandt or a Salvator Rosa than a Guido or even a Greuze. Picturesque though rough, vigorous though incomplete, there is plenty of originality but no refined elegance in this style. Some of the capital letters are very suggestive, but such beauty as they possess appears to be more the result of inherent power than of intention. Manet is evidently one of those sons of genius who disdain the presumed trivialities of our art.

It is to be hoped that the ancient adage, *ludere cum sacris*, will not be applied to us if we venture to insinuate that His Eminence does not indite an exceptionally good style. His letters are perfect patchwork, and would seem to intimate continuous uncertainty, fluctuating as they do from one form to another, in a most vexatious manner. At one moment Cardinal Manning is seen commencing an epistle with a few lines of clear, shapely, and legible letters; then the calligraphy suddenly deteriorates for a few more lines, and then, as rapidly, regains its former respectability. Sometimes his letters are large and sometimes small; sometimes well-made and sometimes mere abortions—dismembered, parti-membered, unfinished. His chief excellence is displayed in careful punctuation and neat paragraphing. The signature is typical of the general mannerism, the capitals being larger, the smaller letters less than the rest of the manuscript, the whole being indicative of a vacillation no mental efforts could keep long under restraint. These remarks, however, refer to the Cardinal's handwriting of some years ago, as we have not seen any specimen of it latterly.

Westland Marston

Dr. Westland Marston's autograph is, in our opinion, not only the best, but also the most literary-looking among our dramatists. Some of his letters are unfinished; they are most unequal in position, dancing up and down like so many goat-footed Fauns, but there is the quaintness of the poet in them. He writes hastily, not too legibly, and sometimes adds a postscript, even when the subject of it has already been fully settled in the body of the communication, but for all that there is an individuality in his calligraphy that proclaims the scribe a man of originality. The author of 'The Patrician's Daughter' carefully heads and dates his letters, but does not punctuate them. His words are too hurriedly ended, and the finals, in the struggles for existence, generally go to the wall. The highest talent, if not genius, might safely be prognosticated of this writer, but a want of care, indicative of fatigability, would seem to demonstrate the absence of controlling persistence.

It is so much easier to detect faults than to discover excellence, that in our search for the former the latter is liable to be overlooked. *Par exemple*, the handwriting of Mr. Theodore Martin is luminous and vigorous in style, but whilst its good quality is apparent, the temptation to dilate upon its shortcomings is strong. The signature, although fairly representative, is more compactly built, and, consequently, better looking than the remainder of his holograph. Its inclination to flourish is equally typical, whilst the chief vice of the style in the union of the final letter of the one word with the initial of its successor is thoroughly exemplified by the *facsimile*. This latter fault is seen running through the whole of an epistle, binding the words together, as if Mr. Martin deemed on the plan of Æsop's old man and his bundle of sticks that that increased their power! But there are some instances where union does not mean strength! Nor is there any evident necessity to shorten or elongate a word to the space left in a line, a Procrustean procedure occasionally adopted by this writer. Notwithstanding these little carpings, the autograph is a handsome, legible, and beauty-loving one, and one, evidently, the work of a man who deems calligraphy a recognisable art.

Joseph Mazzini
___

The handwriting of this pure-hearted patriot must be judged from the standpoint of an Italian chirographist. Doubtless it had been greatly modified by circumstances, and its clarity ofttimes injured by pressure of time. Like the literary men of nearly all European races, Mazzini used the Greek *delta* instead of the less ancient 'd;' his small 's' resembles the somewhat inartistic *sigma* chiefly found among the writers of Latin-descended races when inditing finals, although he, contrary to all custom, uses it even in the middle of words. Mazzini's calligraphy is not fluent in appearance, but suggests the idea of a task, each letter being separately made and quite disconnected from its neighbour. The inditer of such characters as these must have been a man of intense and most concentrated energy—a man whose mind might be expected to be able to grasp the most intricate problems with undeviating force and perspicuity, even the while his frame was on the rack. The autograph is one of the most suggestive in this collection, and might fitly typify the wisdom of the serpent united to the harmlessness of the dove.

It is one of the 'Impressions of Theophrastus Such' that 'wise judgment resembles appropriate muscular action, which is attained by the myriad lessons in nicety of balance and of aim that only practice can give.' It is our impression that those words also describe how calligraphy is perfected, but, notwithstanding 'the myriad lessons,' and the immense practice the author of 'Justice' has had in our noble art, he is still far distant from 'the nicety of balance and of aim' requisite for the formation of a finished handwriting. Monsieur Catulle Mendès is, evidently, not particular about the nature or quality of his stylus—anything between a goose-quill and a telegraph-post will suit his purpose. Sometimes his alphabetical servitors run one way and sometimes the other: his 'J' is, generally, a misshapen 's,' and his 's' is often a *delta* minus its final curve. Most of the other letters are equally grotesque. But all these eccentricities included, the letters of this author are quite legible, strikingly original, and strongly representative of a vivid and fertile imagination. The autograph is written slanting whenever Monsieur Mendès has room for it in that position, and the elegant curve appended is the only attempt he makes at flourishing.

J. S. Mill.

'A judicious reader,' says dear old Montaigne, 'does often find out in other men's writings other kind of perfections, and finds in them a better sense and more quaint expression than the author himself either intended or perceived;' but certainly the reader must be more discerning than we pretend to be if he can make out anything particularly characteristic or masterful in the disappointing chirography of John Stuart Mill. Most of his letters are unformed, straggling in appearance, and anything but suggestive of logical sequence in their war dance over the paper. They are so carelessly constructed that *alpha* might often change places with *omega*, or, for the matter of that, with any other of the vowel signs, without much detriment to the beauty of the epistle. Moreover, though some consonants tumble backwards, others fall forwards; 's' is only an undotted 'i,' 'o' is frequently no better, and the whole array of John Stuart Mill's characters is anything but attractive. And yet, despite their entire absence of elegance, these words are legible, and are utterly free from all clerkly or official taint; nor is it unimportant to note that the signature is the least forcible manifestation in the whole of this writer's autography. Whilst absence of egotism is generally pourtrayed by this final circumstance, the bent of this hand would suggest simplicity—as unalloyed by conventionality—as unadorned by imagination.

From year to year the handwriting of John Everett Millais has varied in style, and has grown more hasty in appearance than of yore, but certain peculiarities have adhered to it through all. One eccentricity is, that after having finished off a note in a fairly legible and picturesque manner, the artist dashes off into 'Yours very truly,' or some kindred expression, in a line of wild flourishes quite different from the preceding chirography, and then relapses into his usual quieter form for the signature—a very good specimen of which is now offered. The calligraphy of Mr. Millais, although formerly somewhat of a literary—of a poetic—type, has of latter years suffered a deterioration in tone—evidently the result of haste—and its early defects have increased in consequence. The most objectionable of these is the frequent stringing together of several words by lateral ligatures, the manufacture of which gives an air of flourish to the manuscript, although really it is—save and except the penultimate line above alluded to—fairly free from that vulgar vice. Although Mr. Millais may not yet have so far surpassed nature in his portraiture as to have realised Lord Bacon's belief that 'a painter may make a better face than ever was,' yet has he given instances of pictorial *expression of the mind* that go far to contradict the great Essayist's dictum, that 'that is the best part of beauty which a picture cannot express.' Nor, all in all considered, is his manuscript unworthy of his artistic perceptions.

Mr. Morris writes as an artist would paint. Although not so careful as Browning's or so startling as Swinburne's, there is great force and characteristicality about the penmanship of the author of 'Jason.' There is a little too much of the bravado look about some of his letters for a poet, which would make one deem their author more likely to be an adventurous seeker after, rather than the harmonious singer of, the 'Golden Fleece.' Many of his down-strokes are very graceful, but there is too much haste and too many contractions in his writing to satisfy the critical taste. His autograph is a fair sample of his handwriting, and there is a peculiarity about it which is probably the result of something more than accident—that is doubtless a piece of artistic affectation—we allude to the two initial letters 'W' and 'M:' one is the counterpart of the other reversed.

The 'French Byron' indited a respectable bourgeoisement kind of calligraphy; of a clear, but not a strongly imaginative, type; legible, but not fantastic enough for a genius, nor quaint enough for a poet. In fact, de Musset's autography is as unlike his presumed prototype's as 'Mardoche' and 'Rolla' are unlike 'Don Juan' or 'Childe Harold.' Of course, the man who made such a stir about *un point sur un i*, dare not omit to dot that letter of the alphabet, nor did he, indeed, frequently disregard any of the *ordinary* technicalities of our Philosophy —within the rules of which are more things than are dreamt of by the herd. But it was in the formation of his autograph that the author of the 'Ballade à la lune' expended the chief portion of his chirographical talents: he varied his signature frequently. The form given in *facsimile* is the rarest, as well as the most interesting, of de Musset's autographs. Sometimes he contented himself with 'Alfred' only, on other occasions he omitted the 'de,' or made such other abbreviations as the whim took him. His capitals were but enlarged copies of the minor members of his alphabet; at times his pothooks and hangers were not uniform in slope; at intervals he indulged in tremendous flourishes, and committed various other scriptorial improprieties. His handwriting scarcely comes up to one's ideal of a great poet's, but it is by no means unsuggestive of such a personage as that recently portrayed with such charm, such love, and such *blindness* by the fraternal pen of Monsieur Paul de Musset.

'Quarrels and divisions about religion,' says Bacon, *'were evils unknown to the heathen,'* and so, doubtless, were pothooks and hangers. *Mais, nous avons changé tout cela*, otherwise there would be no need to congratulate this priest upon his elevation to a cardinalate, any more than this treatise would have a *raison d'être*. Cardinal Newman's manuscript bears some resemblance to Cardinal Manning's, but it is smaller, more legible, more compact, but less English in style than that of his *confrère*. It is carefully indited, from *alpha* to *omega*, without any sign of haste or evidence of faltering, but it is a finical, studied hand, that induces an impression of distrust. *Bonhomie* need not have been looked for in its tortuous little ups and downs, but there is a want of fluency and vigour in these rigid strokes that is far from attractive. The autograph is somewhat larger and scarcely so compressed as the body of the writing, the which, many will deem, more than its author's life, requires an *'Apologia.'*

There is something thin and foreign-looking in the handwriting of the late Mrs. Norton (Lady Stirling-Maxwell). 'Corinne' might have indited such a style of concentrated energy and inexpressible passion as is discoverable in these nervous-looking lines. Original for English writers, a parallel style of chirography amongst Italian and even French scribes would not be difficult to find. It is an irritating, *petite* writing, full of needless contractions—especially in the final syllables—and still more needless flourishes. Although all but the concluding letters of a word are tolerably distinct, the calligraphy is neither well formed nor particularly graceful. The strokes are sloped backwards, but occasionally some of them attain the perpendicular, whilst others follow the natural order, and bend forwards. The authoress of 'The Undying One'—'the female Byron'—latterly indited a much better but less *petite* hand than she did in years gone by, but the unsightly aureole of flourishes round so many of her words detracts from any elegance they may possess. Like many others of her half of the *genus vatum*, Mrs. Norton was fond of underscoring her words. The transient passion, more than the sustained energy of genius, might be predicated from this chirography.

'You cannot read written hand,' was said to the knight in the old comedy of 'The Wild Gallant,' but had he been shown Offenbach's calligraphy, his inability would have been in no way remarkable. The creator of 'La Grande Duchesse' indites the most whimsical, fanfaronading, helter-skelter of pothooks and hangers ever constructed. To strive to analyse the form of his letters would be an idle task. It has been found absolutely requisite, in the autograph, to dock somewhat of the Gargantuan immensity of tail, which, involved as it is from a few skeletonlike scratches, is just the reverse of the good old fable : 'Parturiunt montes, nascetur ridiculus mus.' Is not such a performance thoroughly in keeping with what might have been looked for in the author of such *bouffonneries musicales* as are Offenbach's performances. Unfortunately our hero spoils the fun of his *fantaisies caligraphiques* by making mistakes and rewriting new letters over the old ones, which is about as successful an idea as putting new wine into old bottles : it makes 'confusion worse confounded.' The *on dit* current in Paris is that an unfortunate expert, who had a quantity of Offenbach's calligraphy given to him to decipher, *était devenu idiot à la fleur de l'age*—like the café waiter in Murger's 'Bohême.'

Madame Patti's scriptorial performances are, as regards clearness and general neatness, superior to those of most *prime donne*, but they are not very characteristic. Nevertheless, there is a *petite* beauty—an almost infantile looking simplicity—about the *tout ensemble* of the calligraphy that is attractive. Each separate letter is, as a rule, legibly and carefully manufactured, and would be comprehended if it stood alone—a rare virtue with the chirographical offspring of *le beau sexe*. Nothing very positive need be predicated of such a style ; it indicates little beyond perseverance and artistic care. The autograph of Madame la Marquise does not differ from the other portion of her letters in any marked manner.

The author of the 'Epic of Women' indites a curious style, that rarely varies in kind no matter what speed it may be evolved at. Might we be permitted to resort to entomological phraseology for definitions of the different types of handwriting, we should class Arthur O'Shaughnessy's among the arachnoids, as its slender filaments intersect the page like the threads of a spider's web. It is impossible to deny legibility, grace, and quaint originality to this poet's calligraphy; but the tenuity of its component parts, and their consequent flourishing appearance, gives it a somewhat flimsy form. 'A man's nature runs either to herbs or weeds,' says Lord Bacon; 'therefore let him seasonably water the one and destroy the other.' Mr. O'Shaughnessy's writing, as his poetry, runs to flowers, but he must take heed lest it become too flowery. It is chiefly suggestive, so far as it is idiosyncratical, of ultra-refinement — of nervously appreciative delicacy.

'Ouida's' calligraphy is almost as startling as a sketch by Wiertz; not, indeed, that it is in any way suggestive of the horrors of the artist who painted 'L'Enfant brûlé' and 'Le Soufflet d'une Dame belge.' Heaven forbid it! Its chief idiosyncrasy is the portentous and multifarious shapes of her capital 'Is.' Some are shaped like the figure 7—a figure of mystical import—some like the letter 'J' enormously elongated, and all are weird works of art. Her small 'i' is quite unnoteworthy, is mostly formed like 'e,' and is rarely dotted. The major portion of the rest of her alphabetical capital consists of strings of 'ees.' Two words are all this lady gets into a line, or at most three, stationery evidently being no object with her. She has a woman's weakness for underscoring needlessly, and has a predilection for flourish, the cross of her 't' often reaching from one side of the page to the other. We refrain from commenting upon the symbolism of this manuscript, the autograph of which is a rather favourable specimen of its author's hand, being more compressed than is usual with her.

For a scientist, Professor Owen's chirography is pretty clear. The man who can build up a perfect idea of an extinct animal from its thigh bone only, may perhaps be pardoned if he deem readers able to conjure up an entire letter out of a few helter-skelter twists and twirls. Considerable experience in the decipherment of handwriting causes the great anatomist's to be comparatively easy for us; yet, save the signature—which is much clearer than the body of his letters—Professor Owen's calligraphy is not very legible, and the fact that it is written by a metal stylus does not increase its beauty. When Job desired that his words might be written with an iron pen, he had a reason for it, which our *savants* have not. His capitals are the best part of our professor's epistolary performance, being boldly and clearly formed, but the rest of his writing is small and finical. He punctuates, out, unfortunately, abbreviates, making such unpardonable contractions as 'wh' do duty for 'which,' besides committing other similar scriptorial improprieties.

A very original and characteristic style is Sir James Paget's. Clearly and carefully written, correctly punctuated, and the letters uniformly sloped, most people unacquainted with the tenets of chiromancy might deem this to be the *summum bonum* of styles. Yet it would not obtain much κῦδος from us. Without being feminine, it is too effeminate for our taste, and, with its peculiar alternations of backward dark and forward light strokes, is very confusing to peruse much of. Sir James is rarely betrayed into a flourish, but the abnormal length of his looped letters is very inelegant. This chirographical eccentricity is carried to a frightful extent in the autograph, which is a fair sample of the whole style.

'A damned cramp piece of penmanship as ever I saw in my life,' was Tony Lumpkin's opinion of Marlow's epistle. 'I can read your print hand very well, but here there are such handles, and shanks, and dashes, that one can scarce tell the head from the tail.' Squire Lumpkin, in his tirade against the offending communication, described Mr. James Payn's calligraphy to a t. One stroke waves in one direction, another in t'other; one letter has no top and its neighbour is without a tail; two or three words run into one another, and an entire note is such a complicated, entangled string of scratches, that the reader is fairly bewildered in its attempted unriddlement. No amount of scriptorial pressure will excuse such an utter disregard of the peruser's patience. The finest fancies may be utterly lost, or long overlooked, when concealed in such intricate meshes, and at best only leave an impression of weariness, even as the glasses in the temple of Smyrna represented the fairest faces as deformed and hideous. The signature, although better than the body of the writing, will prove that these comments are not hypercritical, and that, calligraphically speaking, the talented novelist may not claim—he and his hand—to be 'less black than we're painted.'

John Payne's chirography would seem to have had two enemies to contend with: the one esoteric, the other exoteric. The outward foe has driven what would have been a strikingly original style into a professional groove —curbing its quaintness—and the secret force antagonistic to this restraint has caused it to burst out into inordinate flourish. These drawbacks, especially the latter, are much to be regretted, because the author of 'The Masque of Shadows' builds some very beautiful characters, and, as Bacon hath it, 'It doth much add to a man's reputation, and is (as Queen Isabella said) like perpetual letters commendatory, to have good forms.' Mr. Payne's capitals are very bold and striking, and, save in the signature—which is larger than the rest of his writing—conform to all the requirements of the calligraphic art. A fatal facility, akin to what Montaigne confesses to—for when the revivifier of Villon sins he always sins in good company—frequently causes Mr. Payne to run his letters into one another, and by so doing, with one fell blow spoil two beauteous babes. And his flourishes! Contemplating them, and thinking of the valuable time expended upon their gestation, we content ourselves with Rabelais' aphorism, 'Magis magnos clericas non sunt, magis magnos sapientes.'

It is to be feared that those who expect a divulgement of 'The Mystery of the Pyramids' in Mr. Proctor's chiromancy will be disappointed. His handwriting is a neat but something uncertain style of calligraphy that certainly conceals nothing very portentous or marvellous. The author of 'Myths and Marvels' indites a reasonably business-like, literary hand, legible enough for printers and postmen to decipher, and which is suggestive of anything rather than the hieroglyphics of Trismegistus. None of Mr. Proctor's letters are very badly built, and none particularly elegant. They make capital 'copy,' and do not need more than two or three perusals, as a rule, to comprehend. They are more representative—to our notion—of a practised magazinist than of a scientist, but, of course, there may be things not dreamt of in our philosophy hidden in these literary looking 'pothooks and hangers.' The autograph is very typical.

The calligraphy of M. Prudhomme is somewhat small but extremely clear, the autograph being the worst and most careless looking portion of the manuscript. It is in no way suggestive of his namesake's; all *this* Monsieur Prudhomme's alphabetical troops of the line are well manœuvred and well marshalled. Dates, punctuation, and all the minor details of our philosophy are properly executed, and although not so grandiose as Leconte de Lisle's, nor so elegant as Mallarme's, Sully Prudhomme's chirography is both symmetrical and quaint. He makes his 'd' sometimes like the Greek *delta* and sometimes in our *soi disant* Latin form; his capitals—save always in his signature—are correctly shaped, and his finals are carefully and completely finished. But for the puzzling autograph, artistic *form* might be deemed almost innate with such a writer, whilst love of the beautiful must certainly appertain to his nature.

The owner of the *quondam* 'Naboth's Vineyard' indites a hand that might well have excited the wrath of Tony Lumpkin; indeed, 'a confounded up and down hand, as if it was disguised in liquor.' Veritably, it is a provoking style; it looks so clear, vigorous, and, apparently, legible, yet, when inspected, needs a connoisseur to decipher it. If the production of the 'Coming Ambidexterous Man' is to be after such a mode, stately though it look, we shall be inclined to prefer the nineteenth century *homo*, imperfectly digited though he be, as a calligraphical animal. Certainly, if he please, Dr. Reade can write in an elegant manner, and sometimes, as if to prove his capability, he does permit a perfectly formed letter to flow from his trenchant pen; but, as a rule, very few of his letters are properly made. The most defective member of his alphabetical group is the *omega*, the formation of which rarely proceeds further than a single stroke. His 'u' frequently does duty for 'a'—as is exemplified in the signature—his 'i' is often left undotted and his 't' uncrossed; and, altogether, he must not look for much κῦδος from the chirographist. The style generally is of a vigorous feminine type, not unsuggestive of irritability, but fully indicative of its author's powers of doing better—and it is to be hoped that he will, as it is 'never too late to mend.' The autograph is somewhat larger than the rest of the manuscript.

Lord Chesterfield's 'Advice' may never have fallen into the hands of Mr. Sims Reeves, and he may, therefore, be ignorant that, in his lordship's opinion, 'nothing is so ungentlemanlike as a schoolboy's scrawl,' or he would take a little pains to improve his handwriting. His chirography is truly shocking, and what makes this fact more than usually annoying, is our positive conviction that, if he only chose to be commonly careful, he could indite a very respectable style. The signature is even worse than the rest of the epistle, being more cramped, and, apparently, intended to be cancelled by an inordinate, vulgar flourish. Date and punctuation are absent, erasures occur occasionally, flourishes abound, and general carelessness holds high carnival. Little good can be predicated from such writing: nature has evidently, in this case, given the power to produce a reasonable hand, but some ill-disposed fate has nullified it by its manufacturer's want of will.

'Whom the gods love die young,' therefore the brave-hearted artist was torn from life at the very commencement of a brilliant career, without being permitted to drain the goblet of life to the lees. The calligraphy of the young hero is very beautiful, carefully and elegantly formed, and with evident desire to exercise due vigilance over the shapes of the separate letters. Capitals and the smaller members of the alphabet are all properly distinguished from one another, and the *tout ensemble* of the manuscript is so neat, well paragraphed, and punctuated, that it rather gives the idea of a purely literary, than an artistic, man's production. The signature is thoroughly characteristic of the whole style, which is one suggestive of studious care and sympathetic affinity for Art, indeed, all that could be wished for from Henri Regnault.

Although the scriptorial capacity of the late Colonel Richards seems to have been greatly modified by extraneous duty, and the want of form is nearly as palpable as in Tom Taylor's, his writing really is far more carefully finished than that of his dramatic brethren. This one of the creators of the volunteer movement, however, by no means indited a fine hand; his letters look as if a *something* were wanting with them. It is not so much that they need roundness, or that they are 'straggly,' as that they are deficient of any marked peculiarity. The autograph is thicker and displays more energy than the body of his epistles would indicate. The writing is not that of a literary man *pur et simple*, and would rather proclaim an inditer of military manifestoes than the author of 'Cromwell;' but it is fairly legible, and is evidently the handiwork of a man who feels that there is plenty of stamina in him.

Dr. Richardson's calligraphy has not escaped the luckless fate which overtakes the manuscript of most scientific men, although, despite its ill-formation, it is tolerably legible. Why scientists, who know the immense importance of a decimal point, will neglect to dot their 'i,' is a mystery ; and why mathematicians, who cannot fail to recognise the value of symbols, will ignore the use of punctuation, can only be arrived at by a plentiful supply of x, y, and z quantities. These comments are as applicable to the discoverer of 'Hygeia' as to any of his *confrères*. And to such sins of omission and commission must be added feminine angularity, lineal irregularities, and prevalent malformation of his alphabetical offspring. Rickets, spinal complaints, lanky limbs, tottering gait, in fact as many ills as beset a juvenile smoker, encumber the calligraphical productions of Dr. Richardson. The good intent of the writer is apparent, but the means of demonstrating it are startling, not to say distressing.

In estimating the technical value of Madame Del Grillo's chirography it must not be overlooked that, as an Italian, she indites a style very different to what would be expected from her were she English. Ristori's signature, characteristic though it be, is not so well executed as the rest of her manuscript. For those who have the clue to it, her handwriting is decipherable, but it is neither clear nor very attractive, although expressive of a great amount of concentrated energy. Nearly every individual letter is separately formed, or rather, if such a thing dared be intimated of a lady's labour, deformed. As might be expected, punctuation and all the *soi disant* ' minor morals' of calligraphy are completely overlooked, whilst the time which might have been devoted to the acquisition of these strangely ignored accomplishments has been expended in the fabrication of *coils* of absurd and bewildering flourishes.

Christina G. Rossetti

Under the *nom de plume* of 'Ellen Alleyn,' the lady whose autograph this follows made her mark many years ago in the 'Germ,' and it is doubtful whether anything she has since written has surpassed the productions of her youthful years. Miss Christina G. Rossetti's writing —of which this signature, although somewhat larger than the usual run of her manuscript, is typical—at once strikes the peruser as essentially feminine. There is not the slightest trace about it of the Woman's Rights or the Blue—doubtless both excellent things in their way—but from *alpha* to *omega* all is 'pure womanly.' In every holograph of hers which has come under our notice not a single letter is left unfinished, but each one is as perfectly distinct as its neighbour, and all evince quite a pre-Raphaelitishness of execution. Not a single flourish or other vulgarity of Handscript disfigures her writing, whilst the punctuation is all that the most scrupulous chirographist could exact. So much neatness is not always significant of genius, nor of its invariable accompaniment, imagination, and had not the calligraphy of the authoress of 'Goblin Market' had, as well as some blemishes of form, the quality of quaintness to recommend it, it would not have obtained much κῦδος from us. But her manuscript is not faultless, the lines are not even, nor do all the letters slope one way, although this latter defect is not apparent in the more carefully composed autograph. Miss Rossetti omits her dates, and is accustomed to sign herself 'yours sincerely,' or 'sincerely yours.'

The calligraphy of Dante Rossetti is not so graceful as it is original. The manner of both the artist and the poet is clearly discoverable in this handwriting. There is not much fluency, whilst there is a studied—an almost laboured—beauty about it. The sentences are almost always too concise; indeed, Mr. D. Rossetti's letters—so unlike his brother's easy, conversational epistles—appear constrained, and give one the idea of being written by a man who had a task to do, and who would be glad to get done with it. All the letters of his words which should be joined are left disconnected, whilst, as if to compensate for this fault—for fault it is—the poet painter has the habit of running two words into one by Siamese-twin-like ligatures: this is especially observable in the cross of his 't,' which often runs from the top of one word to eke out the beginning of the next. This, it is a pleasure to record, is Mr. Dante Rossetti's nearest approach to a flourish. The signature is fairly typical of the general manuscript, but is somewhat better executed than its author's usual calligraphy.

According to Lord Chesterfield, 'Epistolary correspondence should be easy and natural, and convey to the persons just what we should say if we were with them.' As regards these requirements, Mr. William M. Rossetti's epistles approach perfection, but they are far from attaining the *ne plus ultra* of chirographical lore, in some respects not deserving such praise as Mr. Dante Rossetti's. The artist-poet's calligraphy, whilst lacking the fluency, elegance, and perspicuousness of his brother's, is the more richly endowed with quaintness, a quality which, more than any other, is the invariable accompaniment of the poet—that highest embodiment of human genius. The handwriting before us cannot be denied beauty, but it is as the beauty of a fallen angel : official form and pressure have obliterated much of its pristine impulse, and brought it too near to a certain class type. Nor is it perfect in its class, being sometimes ununiform in slope, and containing—doubtless under high pressure—such inartistic contractions as 'wd' and 'wh.' And Mr. W. M. Rossetti rarely gives the year's date. But these comments seem—save with reference to the last-named omission—to savour of hypercriticism, when one contrasts with the productions of the οἱ πολλοί some pages of this writer's clear, fluent, and elegant manuscript. Amability may safely be predicated from it, and, probably, passionate imagination, compressed and suppressed by the force of circumstance.

Another professor with a scratchy steel pen. Is there necromancy in it, or is an English professor, upon appointment to his chair, compelled to forego the luxury of a quill? Ruskin's calligraphy is, although more *petite*, more legible than that of his fellow *savants*, and yet few of his letters are correctly constructed, and slope in all directions at once. Despite its blemishes, his *Handschrift* is not without a simple, quaint picturesqueness; and, if its author would only deem it worth taking pains with, might become a very characteristic one. Ruskin rarely punctuates, and omits the date of the year, his writing is not free from the vice of flourish, and he frequently runs one word on to the next. In finishing a word he employs nothing but a wild dash to represent the final letters. Eccentricity is all that may safely be predicated of this autography.

George. Aug. Sala.

Shenstone expressed a desire to see some of a certain lady's handwriting, 'in order that he might judge of her temper;' and had he had, as have type-setters, to wade through much *copy* of the general run of manuscript, would, in all probability, have exposed some temper of his own. Mr. Sala's chirography is quite an exception to the rule. It is clear, legible, and almost as easy to read as printing, and, certainly, deserves a testimonial from the printers for its pre-eminent perspicuity. But, beyond its plainness, it possesses little originality of form—no one would mistake it for a poet's. Its leading peculiarity is the replacing the capital 'I,' when a personal pronoun, by the figure 1; the figure being as bare as a pole, without twist, twirl, or loop. No needless flourish disfigures any of his letters, which somewhat resemble schoolboy's 'copperplate' in their exactitude. Punctuation, dating, and all the necessary adjuncts of manuscript for the press, are cared for. Even the rarely noted, but highly valuable distinction between the 'n' and the 'u'—one looping at the top and the other at the bottom—receives due notice from Mr. Sala. The autograph is written somewhat larger than the body of his letters. It seems almost hypercritical to object to such admirable calligraphy, nevertheless, it must be averred that it exhibits little of the beauty appertaining to far less legible styles: it is more suggestive of business capacity than of genius.

The author of 'Indiana' indited a more manly hand than did most of her masculine compatriots: not the affected strained style of a male imitator, or the grotesque antics of a *bas-bleu*, but a veritable virile and vigorous calligraphy. The most salient peculiarity in her writing is the generally unfinished state of the 's,' which, both in the capitals and small letters, is left without any curl or loop—nothing but an upright finger-post. This eccentricity is a modern innovation: in the early period of her literary career, when she wrote a more flowing and less rounded style, 'George Sand' looped her 's' in the most approved fashion. Another peculiarity consisted in underscoring—as if to draw particular notice to them—any surnames mentioned in her correspondence. The signature which we furnish appertains to the last period of her career, and is a very characteristic one—characteristic of her noble heart and mighty brain, as well as of her feminine weaknesses. In the penultimate portion of her life—before she took to the blue ink in which almost all her latter handwriting was done—her autograph was 'G. Sand,' with or without the curious flourish to the final letter, save in legal and literary documents, when the full signature was 'Aurore Dupin George Sand.' It is a very legible and noble style, replete with frankness and originality.

The calligraphy of Monsieur Sandeau is by no means pleasant to peruse ; in fact, only half of it is legible. A curious method which he has of making every letter singly and separately imparts a very grotesque look to his manuscript, and the bad habit he possesses of never completing his alphabetical forms, combined with other undesirable traits, render them far from clear. Jules Sandeau ignores nearly all loops, and, apparently, as much abhors a 'pothook' as Nature does a vacuum, the upward curl of his *delta* being his almost solitary attempt at a curve. His autograph must scarcely be regarded as representative of his general style, it not only being better built, but, in some respects, differently formed. As a rule, this author appears to resort to all kinds of expedients to avoid having to make a loop or twirl. His chirography is by no means commendable.

Of all the vocalists, male or female, whose manuscript has come before us, Mr. Santley's is the best. It is legible, vigorous, and, unlike that of so many of his *confrères*, it is manly looking, A few flourishes disfigure his notes—generally, at the end of each *finále*—but they are not very extravagant, and, with certain needless contractions of words, constitute the most reprehensible items of his chirography. The writing is fluent, uniformly sloped, and the line fairly paralleled. The capital letters —although somewhat mercantile in form—conform to he requirements of calligraphical rules, in being distinct, and proportionately larger than their attendants and followers. In his learned treatise on the 'Science de la Main,' Monsieur D'Arpentigny has sought to prove that every mental organisation is accompanied by a definite form of hand, and from that manual form has assumed to be able to explain the intellectual tendencies. Without dogmatising, our little volume endeavours to show that the *work* of the hand is also typical, and, if this be so, and we read its signs aright, the autography of Mr. Santley—whose signature, by the way, is much larger than the rest of his writing—proclaims an honourable minded, manly person, not over prone to imagination nor deficient in self-esteem.

Poets generally appear to belong to *feræ naturæ*, but from this classification *vers de société* writers should be excepted: they, more correctly, appertain to those creatures catalogued as *domitæ naturæ*. As, however, domesticated animals occasionally manifest signs of savagery, so do these drawing-room bards at times break into rhyme too rich and rare to permit of their exclusion from the veritable *genus vatum*. So with some of Mr. Sawyer's verse; notably do we remember an exquisite Heinesque lyric, 'Nymph and Satyr,' in the little volume 'Ten Miles from Town.' This writer's calligraphy is illustrative of, and resemblant to, his poetry: continuous carefulness, counteracted by unavoidable pressure of duty, has left a very elegant style, but one in which the natural quaintness of the poet has been modified, and his most salient features considerably worn down. Taken from all points of sight, however, Mr. Sawyer's chirography, but for one fatal fact, might not only be pronounced charming, but, almost, everything that could be desirable. The letters are uniform in height, shape, and build, are legibly written, neatly finished, devoid of flourish, and all slope one way, but, alas, that way is backwards! In spite of this defect, Mr. Sawyer's handwriting is one of the most decided as well as most elegant known to us. and compels the mind to believe that its writer will do nothing rashly, nothing unadvisedly, and yet give so spontaneous an appearance to his most matured schemes, that few would imagine them to be anything but impromptu. The autograph is very characteristic of the general manuscript, the fanciful convolutions of the capital 'S' being the only approach to flourish indulged in.

Whether it is a hazel rod that Dr. Schliemann makes use of for the discovery of buried treasures has not yet been divulged, but it is certainly a good quill which he wields in correspondence with his friends. And good use he makes of it! A clear, genial, manly stylus appertains to the finder of 'Priam's Treasure Chamber.' Most of his letters are distinctly and correctly built, whilst some of his capitals are most symmetrical specimens of calligraphic art. His most eccentric sample of the alphabet —the German alphabet, of course—is his capital 'B.' To fully comprehend its curious shape—perhaps modelled on some Hellenic prototype—it must be personally investigated. It suffices, therefore, to note here, that the first down stroke—the stem of the letter—is perfectly straight, whilst the lower loop is brought down as far as the base of the stem and there stops, without being carried up again, as is the usual method. The autograph, being cramped for room, is not so well indited as the rest of the erudite and fortunate doctor's manuscript.

Jules Simon writes in the general commonplace politician's manner, but just a trifle more legible than the majority of his *confrères*. There is little calling for praise in such a style. Monsieur Simon flourishes a little, which is contrary to the habitude of his class. His letters are by no means uniform in slope or form, and manifest no traits demanding special notice. The fearfully elongated caudal appendage is a *sottise* quite unworthy of its author, and the vigour expended over this monstrosity could have been better utilised in supplying the omitted date.

His discovery of Livingstone was, apparently, Mr. Stanley's most conspicuous discovery in the 'Dark Continent.' Whether journalism, civilisation, or the traveller himself, reaped the most advantage from his later expedition, may be left to others to decide. All that needs deciding upon here is our adventurer's calligraphy. It is fluent—fatally so—and looks as if the writer had to get it done before he shot the next rapids: half-a-dozen words are strung together by means of marvellous loops, tied up like true lovers' knots, but contrive to maintain a fair quantum of legibility. Despite its flashy and affected *bizarrerie*, the style is a bold and not unhandsome one, but is not particularly *outré* or original. The idiosyncrasies of such a writer are superficial, and beyond plenty of 'go,' and the ability to make the most of chances proffered by Fortune, little need be predicated of his real disposition.

Stella

It has been said that however a woman may write there is always some peculiarity about her chirography that will betray her sex. An exception to this rule exists in 'Stella's' handiwork. The authoress of 'Records of the Heart' indites one of the most original and puzzling styles in our *répertoire*. It is more like printing than any ordinary calligraphy, and to the poor ill-used printer must appear quite an oasis compared with the desert of bemuddled manuscript he generally has to wade through. To the chirographist, however, 'Stella's' correspondence, although it is dated, punctuated, and, *omen bonum!* entirely free from flourish, will not afford unmitigated satisfaction. Ofttimes her letters are left unfinished, and even those which have their full complement of members are made to slope in all kinds of various directions at once, some backwards, some forwards, and a few, for the nonce, stand bolt upright. Her notes are mostly very brief, and to the purpose, and although their writer has a partiality for underscoring, there is always a reason for it. Apparently written in haste, Stella's notes, to our mind, have a strong under-current of prudence, and are invariably free from all kinds of blots, erasures, and alterations. Corroborative of the prudence indicated by her handwriting is the signature, which rarely runs into a more friendly style than 'yours faithfully.'

'The spirit giveth life,' says St. Paul, 'but the *letter* killeth;' and, without in any way intimating that Mr. Leslie Stephen is of a sanguinary temperament, it must be confessed that there is a mordant air about his 'pothooks and hangers'—his chirographical rapiers and poniards—that is somewhat terrifying. The inditer of this kind of manuscript would have too much self-respect to consciously injure any man, but woe betide the luckless author who, as an author, incurred his critical wrath! There is no breadth, nor roundness, nor quaintness in this writing, but a fretful, cold, skeleton style about it, reminiscent of the hapless Ascians, who—worse off than Peter Schlemil—were born shadowless. Contractions are frequent, 'wh' doing duty for the pronoun, '&' for the conjunction, and so on. Scarcely a letter has its full complement of loops or limbs, all suffering more or less loss in their struggle for existence, or perchance they appertain to a too early stage of evolution. *En vérité*, Mr. Leslie Stephen, your handwriting is not so carefully constructed as to escape the critic's animadversions. You ofttimes forget to cross your 't,' and frequently omit to dot your 'i,' and altogether neglect or ignore the good old precept about minding one's 'ps' and 'qs.' The writing on the whole, however, is fairly legible, and the signature representative.

Richelieu professed to be able to destroy anyone of whose handwriting he could obtain two lines; but he would doubtless have found it a difficult task to make much mischief out of the Rev. C. H. Spurgeon's chirography, so conventional, commonplace, and unoriginal is it. We have been unable to discover one elegantly-shaped letter in all the manuscripts by this gentleman which have come under our notice; from *alpha* to *omega* 'dull mediocrity reigns over all.' His 'pothooks and hangers' so far comply with the first necessity of calligraphy as to be generally, but not invariably, of tolerable legibility, but beyond that they go not. Albeit 'a thing of beauty is a joy for ever,' it is most devoutly to be hoped that things of ugliness—such as these scrawls are—are not destined for so lengthy an existence. If Chesterfield's dictum be true, that 'every man who has the use of his eyes and his right hand' (and both these blessings it is presumed Mr. Spurgeon possesses) 'can write whatever style he pleases,' the writer of this sprawling unformed hand pleases to write only what can but annoy his readers. The signature, it may be pointed out, although characteristic, is better executed than the body of such epistles of Mr. Spurgeon as have come under our notice.

Among English musical composers there is none to equal Arthur Sullivan as a calligraphist. His handwriting is clear, decisive, gentlemanly, to the point, and, although scarcely quaint enough, would not be bad for a poet. The author of 'Trial by Jury' is, however, not faultless as a scribe. Not only is he apt to string two or three words together, but, also, to leave unconnected those letters which should be joined; sometimes, moreover, he slopes them the wrong way, and at other times, but more rarely, leaves them unfinished. His 't' is only occasionally crossed, but in the expressive idiom of *la belle* France, he is careful *de mettre les points sur les i*. The whole style of this writing is characteristic of a man with plenty of 'go' in him, and who, though perfectly *au fait* with what he is about, is none the less careful for that. His signature is more uniform in its slope, and therefore better than the body of his epistles, the which, however, are exceptionally neat for a musical composer.

Mr. Swinburne exercises the presumed prerogative of genius, and writes a wretched hand, although latterly there has been a very marked improvement in it. There is much picturesque vigour, but no beauty, in the formation of his letters, which are probably written during the 'languor of virtue'—at all events, they give one the idea of a painfully laborious work, each syllable being apparently separately formed. There is no straining after effect or vulgar flourish, but his chirography gives one the idea of having been written by a pen that, having served several generations of authors, its owner deemed it sacrilege to cut. A noteworthy feature of Mr. Swinburne's handwriting is his 'i:' it has a very large head and a very small tail, and consequently looks top-heavy. His 'ands' are mere twists, so closely resembling his 'ts' that it requires intense study to tell one from the other. Sometimes he punctuates and sometimes he doesn't. Although full of original peculiarities, his calligraphy, it must be confessed, is cryptographic to the uninitiated. He does not trouble himself about the trivialities of stationery: his envelopes are not fine, nor his paper superfine, whilst crests, monograms, and the whole flunkery of letterdom are completely ignored. As a whole, Mr. Swinburne's calligraphy is one of the few which throw the chiromancer somewhat off the scent: from it he might divine somewhat of the originality, but nothing of the voluptuous beauty and unparalleled music of its author's verse.

The author of 'Edwin the Fair' and 'Philip van Artevelde' seems to belong to the past—at all events, his works have now been relegated to an honourable post among the classics of his country. Sir Henry Taylor writes a very vigorous hand for a man of over seventy years of age; but his words are not well formed now-a-days, although fairly distinct, and have a military rather than a literary look. Erasures occasionally occur. The autograph conveys a very good idea of Sir Henry's usually straightforward style. There is very little beauty, and still less originality about it, and one would not like to predicate much more of it than that the writer was a gentleman. At the present time very few of his letters are regularly formed; there is no dependence to be placed upon any of them, they vary so frequently in style and shape.

Our autograph of one of the most successful living dramatists of England is certainly not a very elegant specimen of calligraphy, but it is far better than its author's general signature. To the uninitiated Tom Taylor's handwriting might suggest the *ne plus ultra* of carelessness, but there are some reasons why it should not be altogether assigned to the limbo of laziness. In the first place he evidently writes too much ; secondly, his thoughts travel faster than his fingers ; whilst, thirdly, in scanning his scrawls one feels that his mind and his pen are not always working in unison : when he is doing one thing he is apparently thinking of another. But in saying this we have said all that we can in favour of Tom Taylor's chirography, for, *en vérité*, fair reader, *entre nous* and the proverbial post, it is, as a rule, simply atrocious, and only readable to postmen, compositors of daily papers, and M. Chabot. Besides all the faults of want of form and finish, of omitted punctuation, and abridged or ignored loops and letters, the author of 'The Ticket of Leave Man' cancels, omits, inserts, and alters words. The *tout ensemble* of his chirography is disappointing ; it does not evince any marked peculiarity of character ; and, if not indicative of having been considerably modified by editorial or official labour, we should have relegated it to the *genus* commonplace.

At a casual glance one might be apt to deem the Poet Laureate's calligraphy anything but legible. On inspection, however, this appearance proves to have been deceptive, and the writing is found to be singularly distinct—at all events for a genius. A fantastic look is imparted to his manuscript by the beginnings and endings of many of his letters being thick or knobby. Indeed, as Shakespeare says, 'the lines are very quaintly writ;' and it is this quaintness, almost bordering on the grotesque, that proclaims the writer to be anything but an ordinary man. The down-strokes are forcibly made, and each letter is carried to its completion with vigour. There is no evidence of weariness or of haste apparent in the finals—the most characteristic signs of this author's idiosyncrasy—they receiving, in contradiction to the usual practice, careful finish. No commonplace character could write as Mr. Tennyson does. His calligraphy is almost all that one would wish that of a first poet of the age should be, and from it one can easily divine the beauty, elegance, and completeness of his works. As a rule, unlike ordinary mortals, he does not write his autograph so legibly, or rather, he makes it more fantastic, than the body of the letter. He writes on good, thick paper, and sometimes omits to add the date. His manuscript for printers is better than his letterwriting, but neither are so good now-a-days as in former years.

Plautus says, 'Sine pennis volare haud facile est,' and usually, a similar deficiency renders writing difficult; but judging from the calligraphy of the late President of the French Republic, he contrived to skim over a pretty considerable surface of paper without pens. What implement Adolphe Thiers did use it would be hard to decide—the Mother of Invention is very contrivative—but the results of his adaptions are anything but attractive and barely legible. For a prescription such a collection of broken-kneed and spavined pothooks and hangers might pass muster, but for handwriting no schoolmaster at home or abroad would accept them. To point out peculiarities of any separate letter would be waste of time, as there is scarcely a single *iota* amongst them but is out of keeping with all rule and reason. Cardinal Chigi boasted that the same pen had served him for three years; but if Thiers really wrote his chirography with anything of pen genus, we deem it must have been the Cardinal's stylus transmitted in unmended condition to his Presidentship. For calligraphical negligence this hand would gain *le grand prix*.

Sir Henry Thompson writes with a quill and not too legibly. With the exception of the preposterous flourishes in the signature, this writing is not only bold, but gentlemanly, and one that evinces complete command of the matter in hand. Fluent and dashing in style, Sir Henry could, undoubtedly, if he chose to take the trouble, indite a very handsome letter, but he will not, at least in his calligraphy, manifest his belief in the good old proverb, 'that what is worth doing is worth doing well.' Who but an expert could arrive at the knowledge that the Christian name in the autograph is intended for ' Henry '? Punctuation is almost ignored by this writer, although, like most of his professional *confrères*, he dates.

Poor Thornbury has joined the majority, but his calligraphy was too remarkable to be omitted from this collection. It has been stated that his manuscript was deemed so execrable by the compositors that they held high festival on his funeral day. It does not appear so bad to us: there are many worse specimens in this book. Indeed Walter Thornbury's handwriting may be styled a very careless copy of Robert Browning's, to whose fine style it bears several points of resemblance; among others, in leaving the separate syllables of a word unconnected; in using the copulative sign & instead of writing the conjunction in full, and in various minor peculiarities. Unlike the greater poet, however, he made his letters in a painfully hurried fashion, as the characteristic autograph shows. Moreover, whilst one of his pothooks stumbles forward another topples backward, whilst a third stands bolt upright, and but very few of them have received their due quantum of limbs. It might safely be predicated of this chirography that but for the modification of surrounding circumstances inciting to haste and heedlessness, its author would have indited a most idiosyncratic and poetic style. Where pressure of outward affairs so alters a man's natural bent, it is scarcely safe to affirm positively, but Thornbury's manuscript, despite all drawbacks, indicates a glowing and poetic imagination, curbed by a somewhat nervous fretfulness.

'Words should be the heart's key,' says the ancient Chinese proverb; but it is to be hoped that a less complicated instrument will unlock the heart of the far-famed chronicler of 'Barchester' and 'Framley' than his *written* words, for they seem suffering from a variety of disorders. Mr. Anthony Trollope is not particularly particular as to the proportion of his letters, some being tall and some being short, quite irrespective of their natural sizes, and none of them being over legible. His 'e' is only an undotted 'i,' and it is only occasionally that his 'i' gets a dot at all, although his 't' frequently gets more cross than it is legally entitled to. His other letters, individually and collectively, are not much better treated, unless we except the capitals, which are frequently built with elegance and distinctness. These strictures notwithstanding, it must be confessed that there is a basis for much calligraphical grace in Mr. Trollope's writing. In fact, with less haste and more care, it would somewhat resemble Mr. Browning's, but pressure of penmanship, official and literary, would appear to have sadly frustrated natural tendencies in this respect; consequently, the chiromancer is thrown off the track, so that little may be predicated of it with security.

In our present list of *savants*, Tyndall's is the only well written signature, and even his autograph is by far the best piece of his calligraphy. It is a picturesque although not a very legible autograph, being in the latter respect somewhat deceptive, a first glance giving the false idea of its distinctness. This feature of the signature is certainly characteristic of his publications. They are so charmingly picturesque, and seem such easy reading, that every peruser fancies he comprehends any scientific topic that the professor chooses to dilate upon. That he does not is no fault of Tyndall's, for his style is perspicuity itself; but unless the reader understands the proposition, all the clearness attainable will not make him comprehend the inference. This professor does not date his letters, and only partially punctuates them; his 'i' is as frequently undotted as dotted, and his 't' is sometimes left uncrossed. Generally his letters are distinctly made, but the final 'y' is scarcely ever more than a scripturesque zigzag; the small 'e' is often made like an 'i,' and the 'o' is but too often the same letter undotted. Erasures occasionally occur, and numerals, when they should be written, are given in figures. As a rule, his 'g' is carefully looped. Some of his capitals are charming specimens of handwriting, and the only attempt at flourish is the somewhat pretentious looking twirl to the last 'l' of the signature. Altogether Tyndall's chirography is by far the best of our *savants*, and, apart from the few blemishes pointed out, happily typifies such delightfully worded works as are his 'fairy tales of science.'

The autograph of Verdi, composer of the two most popular of all operas, 'Il Trovatore' and 'La Traviata,' is ringed by a nimbus of flourishes, and his writing is scratchy, smaller than is usual even with Italians, and is almost illegible. He does not punctuate, but dates; his letters are often disconnected; his 't' is frequently only two lines or scratches crossing each other, and many of his letters vary continually in shape. Although Verdi's epistles are badly and finically written, the final letters are generally made carefully and with decision, the 'e' of the signature being elided in contradiction to his ordinary practice. Underscoring is greatly favoured by this writer, whose calligraphy, although not good as a whole, gives one the idea of a man who warms with his work, finishing off with even greater *esprit* and force than he began.

'Quel beau livre ne composerait-on pas,' exclaims Balzac, 'en racontant la vie et les aventures d'un *mot*?' and he then suggestively traces the *word* through the various phases of its existence, from that point of time when it first became an embodied thought—as a rude hieroglyph—down to its most modern symbol. Herr Wagner, whatever may have been his success in attempting to represent thoughts, words, and deeds by music, has, so far as his calligraphical labours are concerned, not yet arrived at the ultimate perfection of expression alluded to by Balzac. The composer of the Niebelungen Lied's music indites a poor hand, and even when writing German uses the Latin alphabetical forms, or as near to them as he can get. His letters vary continually, and may never be depended upon for two consecutive lines; they are miserable, straggly, scratchy creatures, utterly devoid of grace or vigour. The autograph is typical of the general manuscript, from the construction of which nor beauty nor imagination may be predicated.

Dr. Mary Walker, whom we have taken the liberty of adding to our list of *savants*, may be a charming doctor, but her chirography is anything but attractive, the only adjective by which it can be accurately described being *flashy*. That this lady M.D. should indite a somewhat masculine, or, perhaps, epicene style, is not to be wondered at; but that she should indulge in copying male weaknesses, is a pity. Her style is a forced and unnatural masquerade of the unfair sex. Her flourishes are terrific, and, our space being limited, we have been compelled to amputate a portion of her autograph's caudal appendage. The twists in her capitals are interminable, as, for example, of the 'D' in the signature. Some of her letters slope one way, and some another, and she makes contractions, which are neither needed nor comprehended. However, she punctuates properly, and dates and addresses her communications fully. Her writing is by no means illegible, all the letters being distinctly formed, and her style may be justly deemed a combination of masculine vigour and feminine caprice. The autograph is fairly typical of the general hand.

'Walt' Whitman never writes decently when he uses that modern abomination, a steel pen. No one may hope to write a really good hand whilst using a metal stylus, for it emasculates every virile trait and completely obliterates its user's idiosyncrasies. Surely 'The Good Gray Poet' can have no antipathy to a good grey goose quill, which brings us so much nearer mother Nature than does the forged metallic imitation. Whitman's chirography is not a pleasing nor an intellectual one as a rule, although at intervals, when indited by a flexible pen, it is not without a certain grandeur. His letters are frequently left unfinished; he discards the loops below the line; words are contracted; a twist does service for the conjunction 'and;' erasures occasionally occur, and his manuscript is often hasty and heedless looking in the extreme. Then his 'd' is a rough unfinished kind of *delta* with a wild tailpiece, that, from its size, gives his writing the appearance of flourish, from which abomination it is, however, perfectly free. Lord Bacon tells us 'there is no beauty but hath strangeness in its proportions;' and, certainly, there is as much strangeness in the proportions of some of Walt's words as there is in some of his verse. Yet, for all these strictures, it must be confessed that far more vigour, real unaffected originality, and even masculine beauty, is discoverable in one short hasty note of Whitman's than in fifty folio pages of Bryant's or Whittier's conventional manuscript. Few of the chirographist's minor morals are neglected by the author of 'Leaves of Grass.' He is particular in his punctuation, careful to cross his 't' and dot his 'i,' and is quite *comme il faut* in his correspondence; in fact, shows that there is much method in his (presumed) madness. His signature is generally better executed than the body of his letters, and at times the Christian name of it is shortened to 'W.'

Friend Whittier's manuscript is very vexatious, it varies so wildly. Its leading characteristic is, generally, its very slight indication of any character at all, a seeming paradox explainable by the fact that ruled routine of style has reduced every idiosyncrasy to a dead level of commonplaceness. But occasionally, and this is its most curious trait, Whittier's chirography, like his verse, breaks away from its conventionality, and, as in one instance he indites a 'Maud Muller' replete with truth and beauty, so, in the other, does his autography depart from its clerkly commonplace and display, as if more by accident than design, traces of latent imagination and picturesque beauty. At certain times, also, Whittier writes a terrible hurried scrawl, wherein nearly every letter is formed of tangled loops, like a Chinese puzzle, and the cross of the 't' flashes half across the page. Instead of writing the name of the month, he affects the '1st. mo.' or '2nd. mo.' as the case may be.

Ellen Wood.

Whatever may be deemed of her novels, the chirography of Mrs. Henry Wood is not very sensational, nor even effective; and the autograph, although not much can be said on behalf of even that, is by far the best part of it. Although there is a general air of *vraisemblance* running through the whole of her manuscript, Mrs. Wood's letters are very variable in form and make; in fact, she so frequently changes the shape of the same letter of the alphabet, even in the same epistle, that one is forced to doubt whether it is, as Æschylus says, 'one shape of many names'—πολλῶν ὀνομάτων μορφὴ μία—or a new thing altogether. Her capitals are badly built, and, as a rule, are only the small letters slightly magnified. Sometimes the 'M'—that is, when it takes a fit into its head of beginning upwards from the line—is not without a certain dash of originality, but even then, without the context, we dare defy Mrs. Wood herself to distinguish it from its similarly-manufactured neighbour 'N.' This lady is somewhat given to underscoring needlessly, punctuates but partially, dates occasionally, and, in the *tout ensemble*, induces the idea of a heedless writer.

The chirography of the most popular novelist of the day—most popular if judged by the sale of his works, most unpopular if judged by what is said of them—is not very commendable. It possesses a few negative virtues, for it is not illegible and is not flourishy, but it is not free from vice. We do not so much allude to its sloping all ways at once, nor to many of its letters being only half formed, nor to its utterly preposterous signature—perhaps representative of 'l'Assommoir'—as to the general want of elegance and deficiency of artistic taste. There is an air of *banalité* about Monsieur Zola's handwriting one could scarcely have expected, because, whatever objections may be made to the realistic nature of his famous fiction, its vigour and originality is undeniable. Delicate souls may shrink from unsavoury smells, but it is better for the public to have an open sewer than a covered cesspool. There is nothing calling for praise in Monsieur Emile Zola's autography.

www.ingramcontent.com/pod-product-compliance
Lightning Source LLC
Chambersburg PA
CBHW022118160426
43197CB00009B/1075